104/-

American Marketing
in the Common Market

PRAEGER SPECIAL STUDIES IN
INTERNATIONAL ECONOMICS AND DEVELOPMENT

American Marketing in the Common Market

Vern Terpstra

FREDERICK A. PRAEGER, Publishers
New York · Washington · London

The purpose of the Praeger Special Studies is to make specialized research monographs in U.S. and international economics and politics
available to the academic, business, and government communities. For
further information, write to the Special Projects Division, Frederick
A. Praeger, Publishers, 111 Fourth Avenue, New York, N.Y. 10003.

FREDERICK A. PRAEGER, PUBLISHERS
111 Fourth Avenue, New York, N.Y. 10003, U.S.A.
77-79 Charlotte Street, London W.1, England

Published in the United States of America in 1967
by Frederick A. Praeger, Inc., Publishers

Library of Congress Catalog Card Number: 67-16663

Printed in the United States of America

To my parents

PREFACE

The activities of American manufacturers in the Common Market have become a controversial issue. The Member Countries have an ambivalent attitude toward the American presence, welcoming the benefits brought by these companies but fearing the possibility of an economic Trojan horse. On the other hand, American manufacturers find their European operations increasingly important in their total sales and profit picture.

The primary purpose of this study is to examine the approach of American companies to the continental European market, especially to the EEC countries. The major questions considered are: How do American manufacturers market to these European countries? and, How has the formation of the Common Market affected their marketing approach? There is a secondary examination of the relations between the American firms and the Member Countries of the EEC.

The study was financed by a grant from the Marketing Science Institute in Philadelphia, whose assistance is gratefully acknowledged. Special thanks are due to Professor D. Maynard Phelps of The University of Michigan for his helpful, critical review of the entire manuscript. Finally, the friendly and generous cooperation of numerous executives in the participating firms must be noted. The wealth of data they supplied made this study possible, and the interviews themselves made the research a pleasurable experience.

CONTENTS

LIST OF TABLES

American Marketing
in the Common Market

CHAPTER 1   INTRODUCTION

A marketing program is in one sense the response or adaptation of a firm to its market and socioeconomic environment. Major changes in this environment require a reassessment of marketing strategy if the firm wishes to achieve its goals, such as maintenance or expansion of its market share. In the field of international business, the most spectacular change in recent decades has been the establishment and development of the European Economic Community (EEC). This is significant not only in itself, but as a harbinger of future trade development in other areas of the world. The EEC has been important in part because of its progress toward a customs union, but even more for its impact on expectations, which are so important in business decision-making. As Scitovsky noted already in 1957: "Its popular appeal has generated emotions that may go far towards overcoming the obstacles in its way."[1]

There have been a few surveys in individual European countries on business attitudes and response to the development of the Common Market. A study[2] by the Marketing Science Institute (MSI) was more comprehensive than these surveys, as it involved manufacturers in all the EEC countries except Luxembourg. It included an analysis of the status of marketing in each firm, attitudes toward the EEC, as well as consideration of the firm's adjustments to the EEC.

The present study attempts to analyze and evaluate the Common Market's impact on American manufacturers' marketing activities in the EEC. There are several reasons for a separate study of the marketing adjustments of American manufacturers. First, they do not share the same sociopolitical traditions and influences as their European counterparts. Their views and expectations on European unity tend to be different also.

Second, economic traditions and philosophies on the European continent are quite different from those influencing

1

American manufacturers. This would be reflected in different attitudes and approaches to government, to workers, and,
more importantly, to competitors and consumers. The
European cartel philosophy, paternalism, and product--rath-
er than market--orientation can be mentioned in this regard.

Third, the degree of market orientation and marketing
sophistication of American firms is higher than that generally found in Europe. This was noted in the MSI study,[3] but
it merely reflects a broad consensus of opinion on both sides
of the Atlantic. Two British authors note:

> There is no doubt that the United States has been and re-
> mains the home of the most aggressive distributive tech-
> niques; and it is equally valid to assume that contempo-
> rary fashions in distribution and the techniques which
> accompany them have been voyaging from west to east,
> from the United States to Britain and to the other
> European countries. [4]

Evidences of this contrast in marketing sophistication
are found in the differential role of advertising, marketing
research, and product innovation, as well as in the activity
of professional marketing groups such as the American
Marketing Association. As Scitovsky said: "It may also be
the case that European manufacturers underestimate the flexibility of the European consumer's expenditure pattern; they
certainly have not tried very hard to influence it through price
reductions, advertising, and other such means."[5]

All these factors suggest a different approach to the EEC
by American manufacturers. It is this approach and especially the marketing adaptation to the Common Market that are
the concern of the present research.

REASONS FOR EXPECTING SPECIAL AMERICAN
MARKETING ADAPTATION TO THE COMMON MARKET

The Spotlight on the EEC in
Business Publications and Conferences

The development of the EEC, along with rising discretionary incomes in Europe, has affected the marketing activities
of European manufacturers (though less than might have been
expected according to the MSI study[6]). The basic production--

rather than market--orientation still predominates, though it
is being modified year by year.

Somewhat surprisingly, the Common Market appears to
have gripped the imagination of American manufacturers even
more than their European counterparts.

The large American corporations have seen it as a Common Market or European regional problem more than the
European manufacturers, who considered first the national
impact. This situation prevailed even a decade after the signing of the Rome Treaty and was unhappily observed by a
European economist in November, 1966. He said:

> It is alarming that Americans have recognized the con-
> sumer market potential of the European Economic Com-
> munity faster than the Europeans themselves. Mergers
> and joint ventures in the Common Market are taking
> place more between Europeans and Americans than a-
> mong European corporations themselves.[7]

The European manufacturer is very much the product of
his particular national culture. Being aware of Europe's
traditional divisions, he finds it more difficult to believe in a
true common market or a United States of Europe than does
an American living in the United States, which is the world's
largest common market.

The business press early reflected the interest of American business in the Common Market and, perhaps, accelerated its popularity. Nation's Business, the publication of the
United States Chamber of Commerce, reported the signing of
the Rome Treaty in its May, 1957, issue and called it "one
of the most significant economic events of the twentieth century."[8] The writer suggested that it might require establishment of plants within the EEC.

In June, 1957, Business Week ran a special report: "How
a Single Market Will Change the Map of Europe."[9] The writers
reported the advantages of a single market and saw an Americanization of production and marketing methods.

From the signing of the Rome Treaty, publications aimed
at business management gave regular coverage to the progress
and prospects of the Common Market. They generally stressed
the opportunities rather than the threats to American

manufacturers, especially for those who would establish themselves in the market.

The purchasing power of the unified area may be expected to show a pronounced increase and marketing procedures there will be greatly simplified by uniformity of regulations heretofore determined separately by six different governments. In terms of dollars and cents, the Common Market offers a unique opportunity to American business: United States mass distribution and production skills and management methods, together with our knowledge of high volume, low margin retailing are a natural for a large unified market and are being eagerly sought abroad.[10]

What is found in such articles is the promise of the Common Market. The problems along the way to its realization are not stressed, if even mentioned. The years from the signing of the Rome Treaty to 1960 or later were the time when the Common Market became Topic A in international business. It became almost fashionable to invest in Europe. As early as 1959, an executive reported: "You can't go into a hotel lobby in Europe without stumbling over an industrial investigating team." A European specialist in the Department of Commerce noted also the department's effort in educating business about the Common Market.[11]

Dramatic Increase in American Investment in the EEC

Keynes has pointed out the importance of confidence and businessmen's attitudes in the investment decision. The years since 1957 have been a period when American business investors have had a very favorable attitude toward the Common Market. The McGraw-Hill 1960 Survey of Overseas Operations of U.S. Companies reported: "The most striking development in the regional pattern of overseas investment by United States companies is the shift to the Common Market countries."

The same survey for 1963 reported:

One of the most significant findings of this survey is that an ever increasing amount will be spent for new facilities in the Common Market countries. The amount being spent in this area has increased every year since 1959,

rising from $157 million to over half a billion this year.
It now claims the largest share of the total amount
American manufacturing companies are spending outside
the United States. And the planned dollar amounts rise
steadily through 1965. To some extent, the gain in the
Common Market countries has been at the expense of
other areas of the world. [12]

In 1966, even with tight money and the "voluntary program,"
American investment continued to grow in the Common Market,
according to the survey. [13] The EEC has thus continued to be
the Number One foreign investment attraction for American
business.

It would be wrong to imply that the Common Market is an
Aladdin's lamp for eliciting new investment. Other factors
have also been at work, such as the remarkable recovery and
growth of Western Europe in the 1950's, even before the Rome
Treaty. Another factor that influenced American investment
was the relatively slow growth of our domestic economy in the
early years of the Common Market. It would be equally wrong,
however, to disregard the psychological and economic influence of the EEC on the increase of investment there. This investment increase was foreseen by Scitovsky in his theoretical
study. [14]

The present study is not concerned directly with American
investment in the EEC. The great increase in this investment
does, however, indicate a new American interest in the Western
European market, (or "a near revolution in orientation" as Emile
Benoit called it). The investment data are important as a sort
of thermometer indicating American attention as well as resources allocated to the EEC. The Scripture says: "Where
your treasure is, there will your heart be also." Applying
that to the present context, it would mean a new diligence in
marketing and a probable reassessment of a firm's marketing approach to the EEC.

The spotlight that the Common Market has put on Europe
is one reason for expecting a reappraisal of the marketing approach of the American manufacturer to the EEC. For those
who have made new investment, such reappraisal becomes
necessary to assure its success.

The Growth of the Customs Union and Steps
Toward Economic Union

Another reason for a new marketing approach to Western Europe is the changes wrought by the Common Market as an economic community. Where there were four separate markets (considering Benelux as one unit) with separate tariff walls, there is rapidly developing an internal free trade area. Internal tariffs had already been reduced by 60 per cent by July 1, 1963, and in 1966 were only 20 per cent of their pretreaty level. While other barriers yet remain, remarkable progress has been made toward the establishment of a customs union with a free trade area internally and a common external tariff. The promise of this large common market is a magnet drawing American manufacturers. It should have an important impact on their marketing approach to the EEC as a whole rather than to separated national markets.

The Rome Treaty program for eliminating nontariff barriers and for approximating or harmonizing national regulations affecting trade reinforces the approach to a true common market. This will further encourage a market-wide strategy. Although little progress has yet been realized on these nontariff matters, there is still promise for the future.

New and Stronger Competition
in the Common Market

Another factor requiring new marketing strategy is the increase in competition in the EEC. The easy sales of the early postwar period are past, and European manufacturers are now well able to compete. This means a greater struggle for markets and, therefore, more emphasis on marketing and on winning buyer approval. The need for and difficulty of attracting the consumer are reinforced by the buyers' market now prevailing generally in Europe.

USEFULNESS OF THE STUDY

A study of American manufacturers' marketing adaptations to the EEC can be useful on several counts. It will add to our understanding of the large American firm as an adaptive international organization. The Darwinian idea of adaptation for survival is recognized by businessmen, too, even in the international sphere. According to Ray Eppert, president of Burroughs:

International trade is rapidly reaching the point where
the products and competitive status of a United States
company must be rated on an international basis.   The
reason is simple--if the company can't compete in the
world market, it is only a question of when it will not
be competitive in the United States. . . . If there is any
certain receipt for failure, it is that marketing management should be isolationist and ignore the world market
in the naive belief that the U. S. territory is big enough.
That is the perfect way not to capitalize on the rapidly
growing world market and to lose the United States market as well.[15]

Such a study will also be useful for the American manufacturer contemplating new marketing operations in the EEC.
What problems will he encounter?   What practices and policies are appropriate?

The study can be of interest even to firms already there.
When we're not sure we have all the answers ourselves, we
like to consult or observe others in similar circumstances.
Example: A recent interview showed that one firm with EEC
plant investment since 1959 had sent a team to consult with
another firm with longer EEC experience concerning plant
location and related matters for a new plant to serve the whole
Common Market.   Both have total sales of well over $1 billion.

Consideration of the operations of other American manufacturers in the EEC should be helpful to a firm in evaluating
its own performance there.   While profits are an important
gauge of business performance, a comparison of the behavior
of other firms in a similar situation is also valuable to management in a world of uncertainty and imperfect knowledge.   Peer-
group comparisons are important not only in individual psychology.

In a world where common markets and free trade areas
are multiplying, the American experience in the European
Common Market should further provide a useful background
for marketers to similar areas elsewhere.   Obviously, many
factors will be peculiar to the EEC; but other findings should
have a more general validity, just as economists apply the
theory of economic integration to the various experiments
around the world.

RESEARCH METHOD

The over-all goal of the study is to analyze the marketing adjustments of American manufacturers to the European Common Market. The purpose is not merely to describe, however, but rather to posit first the types of adaptation to be expected in a common market and then to analyze actual adjustments in the light of these expectations or hypotheses. In formulating hypotheses as to the anticipated marketing adaptation to the EEC, the author drew upon two major sources: the economic theory of customs union and the development of marketing practice in the United States, the leading common market.

The terms "marketing adjustments" and "adaptations" are used here to indicate changes made by a   firm in response to stimuli on the demand or market side of its operations rather than from technological or supply factors. Using the term "marketing" in this somewhat broad sense, the following types of activities and adjustments are included:

1.   Location of supply (production) for the Common Market.

2.   Product policy, including product line, product planning, and standardization.

3.   Promotion, including advertising, branding, packaging, warranties, and personal selling.

4.   Marketing research.

5.   Pricing policy.

6.   Distribution policy and practice.

To examine these adjustments, a before-and-after picture is desired: What was the American manufacturers' marketing approach in 1957 (pre-Common Market), and what is their marketing approach today? To the extent possible, such a dual picture is presented. Actually, however, there is more space given to the current picture, with an explanation of the changes that   have occurred.

Since most of the material needed for this research has not been published and is often of a confidential nature, it had to

be obtained directly from American manufacturers marketing
in the EEC. It was necessary to question the people involved
in the marketing decisions to understand what has taken place
and why.

The Sample of Firms

The ideal is to obtain a complete and representative picture of the marketing adjustments of American manufacturers
to the EEC. The universe should consist of manufacturers
marketing in the Member Countries before 1958 and continuing up to the present. Interrogating such a universe presents
serious problems, however. A mail questionnaire could get
wide distribution, but experience has shown that the proba-
bility of cooperation in a lengthy mail questionnaire is very
low. A manageable random sample for personal interviewing
would raise questions as to representativeness. It may be
that the most accurate picture of current practice is given by
the activities of the major manufacturers.

Because of these considerations, the procedures used in
selecting the sample were as follows:

1. It was decided to include only very large manufactur-
    ing firms (of a size to fit into Fortune's 500). In the
    absence of specific data on individual American manu-
    facturing operations in Europe, it was felt that the
    larger American operators in the EEC are the same
    manufacturers who are important in the American
    market. Data on EEC sales and investment as a per
    cent of the firms' total tend to support this. A study
    of McKinsey & Company, Inc. showed that one hun-
    dred major United States corporations have over one
    half of the total United States corporate investment
    overseas.[16] The larger firms not only have bigger
    operations in the Common Market, but also better
    staffing and information available to be useful respon-
    dents. Finally, the delineation of the activities of
    large firms is apt to give a more representative
    picture than the same number of small firms.

2. The number of firms to be interviewed was set at
    twenty-five. The important variable of nationality is
    not present in this study as all the respondents are
    American. Besides nationality, the major variables
    in the MSI study turned out to be the particular branch

of industry (pharmaceutical, automotive, electrical, etc.) and the market served (consumer versus industrial). With such a few variables, it was felt that a sample of twenty-five large firms would give adequate coverage and representation of the major patterns of American manufacturers' marketing adaptation to the EEC. Of course, time and cost constraints were also considered.

3. The twenty-five firms were to be divided evenly between consumer nondurables (ten firms) and industrial goods (ten firms) with five firms in consumer durables. A further guide to broad representation was the tenfold industrial classification used in the McGraw-Hill survey on overseas capital expenditures of American companies.

Further information on the actual sample is given in Appendix I.

The Interviews and Respondents

Because of the inadequacies of a mail questionnaire for the present research, the approach taken was to prepare an extensive interview guide to be used in personal interviews. Since the experience of each respondent was different, each interview had to be adapted to fit the particular situation. With the prepared interview guide, this was possible without sacrificing consistency. The unique experience of a firm could be investigated without omitting the over-all picture. Most of the interviews took place in 1964. Additional data were gathered in 1966.

Because the information required dealt with policy matters and operations outside the country, the respondents had to be in high positions of responsibility in their firms' international activity. Some indication of their European involvement is given by the fact that almost one fourth of them were in Europe when the initial contact was made. Two of the vice-presidents were European; and five other respondents had lived in Europe for at least two years, working in their firms' European operations. Although the interviews were primarily with one representative of the firm, a total of forty-nine people were interviewed in the twenty-five firms. In twelve firms, a vice-president was the principal respondent (four were also company directors). The others had a wide variety of titles, but all were in responsible positions in international operations.

NOTES TO CHAPTER 1

1. Tibor Scitovsky, Economic Theory and Western European Integration (Stanford, Calif.: Stanford University Press,
1958), p. 9.

2. Marketing Science Institute, Marketing Development
in the European Economic Community (New York: McGraw-
Hill Book Co., Inc., 1964), pp. 1-5.

3. Ibid., p. 26.

4. Nicholas A. H. Stacey and Aubrey Wilson, The Changing
Pattern of Distribution (London: Business Publications Limited,
1958), p. 337.

5. Scitovsky, op. cit., p. 122.

6. MSI, op. cit., pp. 98-126.

7. "U.S. Payments Efforts Causing Tight Money in Europe," The
Wall Street Journal, November 9, 1966, p. 9.

8. "How's Business? Today's Outlook," Nation's Business,
XLV, 5 (May, 1957), 42-43.

9. "How a Single Market Will Change the Map of Europe,"
Business Week, June 29, 1957, pp. 70ff.

10. "Your Share of Europe's Markets," Nation's Business, XLVII, 12 (December, 1959), 88.

11. Conversation with the author, April 16, 1964.

12. "The Push Overseas Keeps Going Strong," Business
Week, September 7, 1963, pp. 27-28.

13. "The Growth Slows Just a Little," Business Week,
August 6, 1966, pp. 36-38.

14. Scitovsky, op. cit., p. 44.

15. Parlin Award Lecture, Philadelphia, May 19, 1964.

16. The Philadelphia Inquirer, November 11, 1963, p. 24.

CHAPTER 2 — LOCATION OF SUPPLY

We have suggested that a marketing program is a response of a firm to its environment. There are many things a firm can do in attempting to adjust to, or control, or modify its market environment. In the case of the Common Market, a basic marketing consideration is how the market shall be supplied. Many of the marketing activities discussed in later chapters depend importantly on the decision made as to market supply.

There are two aspects to the question of location of supply for the EEC. The first is whether to supply from the United States or from within the Common Market. The second arises after a decision has been made to produce in the EEC: Should there be national plants or centralized production for the whole Common Market?

There are several reasons for expecting an increase in American production within the EEC. The formation of the customs union means that there will be no tariffs on goods produced in one Member Country and sold in another, whereas exports from the United States will face the common external tariff. Thus, there is a strong incentive to get behind the tariff walls and enjoy free trade in all six Member Countries, rather than trying to surmount tariff and transportation costs by exporting from the United States.

European recovery is another factor encouraging local supply. This works in two ways. First, on the demand side, European recovery has meant rapidly rising incomes, which have made Europe a more attractive market than ever before. Increased wealth reinforced by economic integration suggests that local production can now be large-scale and profitable. On the supply side, European recovery has meant strong local competition for American manufacturers selling in Europe. Subsequent to World War II, America was frequently the only source of supply; and exporting was not difficult. The picture has now changed greatly; and many manufacturers will find that local production, with its possibilities of adaptation of

products and techniques, is the only way to meet competition
and maintain a market share.

Various other factors encouraging European production
will be mentioned briefly. The great amount of publicity about
the Common Market is   one favorable element. The relative slowdown in the United States economy after 1957 is
another. The prestige or fashion element in going international by producing abroad is an intangible but positive
influence.

As to location of manufacture within the EEC, the major
expected development would be centralization of production.
With the internal free trade area, logic would suggest placing
plants to serve all the Member Countries regardless of previous national boundaries. There can be contradictory forces
here, however. Where transport costs are important or where
marketing considerations require adaptation to national markets, production could be more on a national than on an EEC-
wide basis. Furthermore, the customs union will take some
time before it is completely realized; and there is the additional problem of harmonizing diverse national laws that
affect trade flows as much as do tariffs. For firms with several national plants when the EEC was formed, the expectation would be for rationalization of production and specialization by plant.

Thus, the two developments expected concerning location
of supply are increased American manufacture within the EEC
and a trend toward centralized production for the whole Common Market.

INCREASED MANUFACTURE
WITHIN THE EEC

A major impact of the Common Market has been to influence location of supply for Europe. European integration was
one of the principal factors drawing the attention of American
business to the Old World. Benoit wrote in 1961: "The number of American companies investigating direct investment
possibilities in Europe has been so large as to imply a near
revolution in the orientation of U.S. business."[1]

What are the reasons for the great increase in American direct investment in Europe? The answer given in the McGraw-Hill survey is "new markets." It is not clear what this means, but it suggests that the Common Market is somehow new or different from what existed before and is consequently more attractive. The fact that this new market is drawing investment means further that it is to be reached, at least in part, by local production. Thus, the "revolution in orientation" mentioned by Benoit has two aspects: first, a great increase in American business interest in the European market; and second, a decision by many to serve that market by producing locally in addition to or in place of exports.

The experience of the respondent firms will be useful in analyzing the new pattern of production and supply for the Common Market. Since the primary goal of this study is the analysis of marketing adjustment to the EEC, one of the sample requirements was that respondent firms had been selling to Western Europe before 1958. In all cases, however, there has been a great increase in attention to and investment in the EEC. While nineteen of the companies were selling to Western Europe (sometimes just to England) before World War II, only eight were manufacturing on the Continent then. The remaining seventeen had begun direct operations or licensing since 1945, and eight of these started in the Common Market after the signing of the Rome Treaty.

Table 1 (Page 15) shows the strong trend toward supplying the EEC from local production. Whereas less than one fourth of the companies placed 95 per cent reliance on European supply sources in 1957, over half of them did so in 1963. Furthermore, all the remaining firms had great increases in production in the Common Market; and several mentioned that the per cent of local supply was growing steadily. It should be noted also that this higher per cent is on a much larger base of EEC sales so that the absolute figures would be more impressive. This trend has continued into 1966; but the rise has been less spectacular, and the figures are incomplete.

One aspect of the growth in European supply is the multiplication of countries in which manufacturing is done by an individual firm. Table 2 (Page 15) shows the picture at the end of 1965. The twenty-five firms had a total of eighty-eight country production sources; i.e., the average firm was pro-

TABLE 1

LOCATION OF SUPPLY FOR THE COMMON MARKET

Per Cent Local Production	1957	1963
95% or more local production (including licensing)	6	13
50-94% local production (including licensing)	9	8
less than 50% local production (including licensing)	10	4
Total Firms	25	25

TABLE 2

NUMBER OF MEMBER COUNTRIES IN
WHICH FIRMS WERE PRODUCING, 1965

Member Countries	Number of Firms	Member Country Sources
1	2	2
2	3	6
3	7	21
4	6	24
5	7	35
Total	25	Total 88

ducing in more than three different Member Countries. (The number of plants was much higher than eighty-eight, as several firms had more than one plant in the countries where they were manufacturing.)

There was no particular pattern except that all of the firms manufacturing in two countries or less were consumer goods firms. All ten of the industrial marketers were producing in three or more countries. There was some tendency for the older firms in the market to be manufacturing in more countries, although two of the oldest were in just two countries and two of the newer ones were in five countries. Some firms had plans for building plants in yet more Member Countries, and others were negotiating for acquisitions. This was an interesting development because one would expect a concentration rather than a dispersal of production in a common market. This is discussed further in the chapter on distribution.

In 1957, the same firms had a total of fifty-six Member Country sources versus eighty-eight in 1965. Thus, more than one third of these were added since the Rome Treaty was signed. This was in addition to expansion of facilities or new plants in countries where production was already occurring. For twelve firms, expansion took place entirely in the countries where they had started, whereas the other firms added a total of thirty-two Member Country sources. Eight of these were beginning their first production within the EEC, while the other five were expanding to other Member Countries.

These figures indicate the geographical spread of production by American manufacturers and something of their strategy in approaching the EEC. However, the most common measure of business interest in the Common Market is the volume of direct investment there. This does not reveal some aspects shown by the other indicators above, but it is important in showing the increased attention to the EEC. Where the treasure is, the heart is also.

Investment Indicators of Local Supply

This study obtained little data on the increase in investment in the EEC. The McGraw-Hill survey cited earlier covers this matter well. However, the increase in local production sources just discussed is related to the investment pattern, since new production means new investment unless it is by licensing, which has not been the usual case.

Ten of the respondent firms had no investment in the EEC countries in 1957. One still has none, as it operates by export and with an Italian licensee. The other nine have built or ac-

quired plants or entered into joint ventures, often acquiring
equity in a licensee. The fifteen firms with previous investment have all expanded it. This expansion has taken various
forms--new plants, expansion of existing facilities, acquiring or expanding equity in joint ventures. The trend is definitely toward greater ownership of European operations.
A study by Booz, Allen & Hamilton Inc. reports the same
trend on a global basis. [2]

For a third of the firms, no answer was received as to
the relation of Common Market and American investment.
For another third, EEC investment varied from 1-10 per cent
of that in the United States; and for the last third, investment
in the Six equalled from 11 per cent to almost one third of
investment in America. This is a further, though incomplete,
sign of the significance of local supply for the Common Market. It is incomplete because it does not include local manufacturing carried on by licensees; and this still accounts for
an important part of the European supply for a number of
firms, especially in the industrial market. For example,
one chemical firm had just one wholly owned operation, but
several joint ventures and about twenty-five licensees throughout the EEC. Another industrial marketer had greatly expanded
local output with relatively little investment through a three-
fold program: (1) It specialized its three plants on a product
basis; (2) it automated operations in these plants; (3) it did
more subcontracting of components.

Investment data are further incomplete as to the importance of local supply because they account only partially for
joint ventures. For example, two consumer goods companies
operated exclusively on a joint basis with an average of fifty
per cent ownership. At least ten more firms operated in
part with joint ventures. Very few operated exclusively on
a 100 per cent ownership basis. A "pure" type of
ownership basis is hard to find in the large firms operating
in the EEC. For example, where manufacturing facilities
are 100 per cent owned, there may be joint ownership
in local assembly or distribution operations where global coordination is less important than in manufacturing.

Changing Role of Exports

The converse of the new role of local supply is the changing position of exports. For the six firms with 95 per cent or

more local supply in 1957, exports were then and are now almost negligible. They consist of specialized components or
ingredients, such as color for nail polish, or a particular product with limited demand in the market. Some of these firms
had products where transportation costs prevented serving
the market from the United States. In these cases, it was
local supply or none.

For the nineteen firms where export was a more important means of supplying Europe in 1957, seven have gone almost
completely over to local supply, and all except one of the rest
have increased European provision both absolutely and relatively. This increase in local production was not necessarily
at the expense of exports, as was feared. Actually, only ten
of the firms had a decrease in exports to the EEC (occasionally these exports were from United Kingdom plants). Nine
had increases, including a number who multiplied several
times their 1957 sales volumes from America. Only one industrial marketer had a decrease in exports to Europe. Only
two consumer goods firms had an increase. It appears that
being "in the market" is more important in consumer goods
than in industrial goods, where technological factors are relatively independent of local market differences.

Firms that had increased exports from the United States
frequently credited the boom in Europe for this. However,
most firms had also devoted more attention and personnel to
European sales, either in the United States or in a European
sales-and-service agency. Some companies discovered after
establishing a European plant that it was at the same time an
ideal base for promoting United States exports. Occasionally
in its annual report, a firm claimed that its major emphasis
was still on exports from America. This seemed to be partly
a public relations affair related to labor relations ("exporting jobs") and balance of payments difficulties.

Along with the changing relative importance of exports,
there is often a change in their composition. Where exports
are down, finished goods manufacture is generally now carried on in Europe with specialty items, parts, or ingredients
imported from the United States. For example, instead of
finished goods, one paper products firm exported used
machinery from the United States for setting up local production. It found it could still be competitive in Europe with

these machines, while the newer ones it had developed were
more necessary in the more demanding United States market.

Even firms having an increase of exports usually found
them different in nature. An electrical firm found consumer
products becoming more important as European housewives followed their American counterparts. A drug and some chemical producers were compounding or finishing many goods in
Europe, although still supplying some basic raw materials
from America. The "bread and butter" staples were disappearing from the export list because there was a good market
in Europe for them and they were being manufactured
locally or else European competitors had taken them over
and made them unprofitable to the American firm.

Technological development strongly affects export composition. Obsolescence eliminates some products, technically
advanced European firms take over others, and the newest
results of American research and development make up the
new volume. This is especially true for such product groups
as business machines, chemicals, and materials-handling
equipment. Whereas products experienced shorter lives in
the American market in the 1950's, this is now commonly
occurring also in Europe. Hans Horms, chairman of the
board of a large German pharmaceutical house, complained:
"Prior to World War II, it was generally possible for a product to be sold at a satisfactory profit for fifteen to twenty
years. Today, everyone is happy if a new product can be sold
profitably for five years."[3] He cited the American presence
as one important causal factor.

Reasons for Growth in EEC Supply Facilities

The increase in Common Market production sources,
investment growth, and the changing role of exports have all
been considered as facets of the new importance of local
supply in marketing to Europe. They are varied evidences
of the fact, but they do not explain why it has occurred.

Many factors motivated the initiation or expansion of
manufacturing facilities in the EEC. Some of these factors
were mentioned at the beginning of this chapter. They were
selected primarily on the basis of a priori reasoning. As
a result of the study, a more complete explanation can now

be given. For convenience of discussion, the factors are
grouped into four categories. These categories are: economic
reasons, political reasons, marketing reasons, and other
reasons.

Economic Reasons

Many economists consider integration's effect on investment as its most important result. It is true that the formation of the customs union with the threat of tariff discrimina-
tion was an important factor in the decision to invest (produce)
in the EEC. Few of these new plants can be called "tariff
factories," however, in the sense that this consideration was
the only reason for their establishment.

The tariff factor was important for some companies that
had begun manufacturing in England in the mid-1950's. When
Britain did not join the EEC, plants were opened on the Continent. Most frequently, though, the threat of tariff discrimi-
nation was only a contributing rather than major consideration.
For an industrial concern that served Europe both by licensing
and exports, the reaction to the EEC was not to set up direct
manufacturing, but rather to open a sales-and-service agency
in Switzerland to protect its export business. Several years
later the firm did begin direct investment because of its desire
for more active participation in profitable markets. Some
firms considered local manufacture as a way to protect exports.
While they found the nature of exports changing, export volume
could be sustained or expanded in conjunction with local plant
operation. A drug firm used local manufacture as a pilot operation to determine relative costs in Europe as a basis for de-
ciding which products to make locally and which to ship from
America. This approach, unfortunately, is not available to
all manufacturers.

Another economic element related to integration is the
opening up of a market of 170 million people where the largest
single market available before was just over 50 million. The
purchasing power is second only to the United States. "It's
like having another whole new U.S. market open up," said one
executive.

New competition in the larger market was an important
consideration to many firms. At an American Management

Association convention on the Common Market, George Ball
warned the delegates: "Once European producers have ad-
justed their operations to the scale of the Common Market,
it may be extremely difficult to set up a competitive source
of production within the EEC."4 Several firms mentioned
this need to defend their European markets by local manufacture, against American as well as European competitors.
One said: "If you're not in now, you probably won't be able
to get in ten years from now. Volume is so critical that
you can't let a competitor get a better position in the market." One firm reacted to increased European competition
by a fairly typical approach: reorganizing and enlarging
the international division, opening new sales offices in
Europe, and acquiring local manufacturing plants.

Even outside the European market, the American manufacturer must be concerned. First, he must think of third
markets where strong new European competition is encroaching. Then for some products he must even consider threats
to the domestic market. For example, foreign automobiles,
typewriters, sewing machines, and cameras play a role in
the American market that would have been inconceivable a
decade ago. As one executive put it: "If the company
cannot compete in the world market, it is only a question of
when it will not be competitive in the U.S." Establishment
of local operations in such important markets as the EEC
strengthens the entire global posture of an international
company. A Department of Commerce study in 1965 showed
that the exports of American manufacturing affiliates in
Europe were $3.6 billion in 1964, and that total sales of these
affiliates rose $2.5 billion in 1964 alone.5 It seems that the
best defense is a good offense.

There are several other economic inducements to local
manufacture that are not directly related to integration.
Internal taxes are on an f.o.b. basis versus c.i.f. on imports.
Transportation costs are greatly reduced. Labor costs are
generally less in Europe, though some respondents found no
savings in this regard. As to other costs, an executive noted:
"It is a market for products whose big costs of R and D, processes, and plant design are already paid in the U.S." When
many investment decisions were being made, there was still
a lack of currency convertibility in Europe. Inconvertibility
encouraged reinvestment of earnings accumulated there, as
well as discouraging dollar imports.

Another and perhaps primary economic attraction is "new markets." Both European recovery and the profit motive enter in here. The slowdown in the United States economy after 1957 helped to make Europe look relatively more attractive. European recovery started long before the Rome Treaty was signed, of course, but as one respondent noted: "The Common Market made us aware of the market potential in Europe."

As one aspect of the "new markets," several consumer goods firms saw Europe going through the same type of consumer revolution that the United States experienced in the 1920's and the 1930's. A number of both consumer and industrial goods companies expect their international divisions to be as big as their domestic divisions by about 1970. For a few firms, it is true already. One executive said: "If we hadn't decided to expand overseas in the mid-1950's, we would be in less than half the free world markets and out of the growth areas." Thus, the traditional profit motive was a force for establishing and expanding operations in Europe.

Political Reasons

Political considerations are not primary to the investment decision, but neither can they be ignored. Such elements as government stability, antitrust attitudes, and nationalistic purchasing must be investigated. The formation of the Common Market augured well for the political dimension. It promised a more definitive end to civil war in Europe and a greater harmony and stability in government actions. One executive even said: "The European market is more stable than the United States. For example, concerning antitrust, they're more friendly and pragmatic. It's a generally favorable government climate." DeGaulle has not improved the climate, however; and government attitudes cooled a bit in the mid-1960's.

While much progress has been made politically, the "United States of Europe" is not just around the corner. Nationalistic preferences and purchasing are still strong in some areas. Manufacturers of such products as drugs and major electrical equipment are especially affected by these preferences and usually have to be established in a particular country to sell there. This is an inducement to local manufacture, but on a national basis rather than on a rational basis for the whole

Common Market. Diverse patent laws are another problem
to whose solution progress is being made. A whole range of
national taxes and regulations concerning business is scheduled
to be standardized eventually, further facilitating local operations.

Marketing Reasons

There are strong marketing reasons for establishing
European manufacturing. These are related to customer service, market information, product policy, and distribution.

In a free market, the customer must be persuaded to buy
a product. If there are many persuaders, the task of attracting the customer becomes difficult and complex and usually
requires local operations to be done effectively. A study of
the electronics industries showed that for customer service
manufacturing facilities located in Europe had an important
advantage over United States facilities, both in selling and
servicing the customer. [6] Where product adaptation or customer service is needed, the respondents invariably came
to the same conclusion: A European manufacturing source is
more effective and can often help with United States exports
as well.

When a manufacturer is producing in the market, he
can know and service local customer wants better than through
exports. These customer wants are rarely the same as in
America. Not only that, there is still diversity among national
markets in Europe. An economist with one respondent firm
said: "The great barrier to our exports from the United
States to the Common Market is not the tariff but the lack of
homogeneity in the market." This problem is greater in the
consumer market.

Customer confidence is increased with local manufacture.
One executive asserted:

It's largely a matter of confidence. We could export,
but a customer buying on this scale wants to deal with
manufacturers rather than agents. By establishing a
factory to make some of our products in Europe, we can
show him we're in business there. He can walk through
the plant and see the operation. By then, it's of no concern to him that most of the components are imported.

The question of confidence is more pertinent for industrial marketers.

Better market information is another reason for local operations. In a competitive market there is a need for rapid market feedback. With the new competition in the Common Market, the more immediate the physical presence of the producer, the more likelihood of good market information to guide operations. This presence can provide not only feedback on changing customer needs and desires, but also knowledge of competitors' actions and products. A few respondents had research labs in Europe whose purpose was as much for study of competitors' products as for their own research needs. In the electronics study mentioned above, it was found that "the greatest advantage in European operations is an intangible one related to familiarity with the market."

Product policy can be more effective with European manufacturing. A logical corollary of better market information is the development or adaptation of products that in turn give greater customer utility. If a significant market penetration is desired, there is usually a need to make or adapt products for the market (especially in consumer goods). This is done best within the market where the local needs are not a fringe consideration as is often the case with exports. Most of the consumer goods companies were making products that were adapted to the European market (or even to national markets). This was also true for over half of the industrial marketers. While adaptation of products is usually the first step in local manufacture, there will often follow production of new products especially for the European market--products that have no market in the United States. This becomes a European rather than an American or export product strategy and is most consistent with long-run market goals.

Pricing can be an aspect of product adaptation, also. With local manufacture of consumer goods, the lower price is likely to permit greater market penetration. A manufacturer of specialty food products had only a "carriage trade" through exports, but was greatly expanding coverage with the lower-priced local products. Another respondent said: "We have to establish local plants to be competitive locally. We need a low shelf price to get volume for profitable operations."

A further aspect of product strategy in local manufacture
is the possibility of expanding the product line. On an export
basis, sales are primarily of specialty items or star performers. With local production the product line can be expanded
to cover other goods that would not be competitive as exports. Once the leading products have opened the door, the
rest of the family can follow more easily.

Distribution can be improved with local manufacturing
facilities. One respondent said that for their line it is necessary to manufacture in France to get distribution in France.
The wholesalers did not want to handle a product not manufactured locally. Others who do have distribution often find that
the close supervision and contact of local manufacturing im-
proves performance. Distributors' morale and loyalty are enhanced when this more permanent commitment is made by the
manufacturer. Furthermore, the greater volume and broader
line of local manufacture may attract better distributors or
enable a more efficient method of distribution. A food firm
gave as one reason for manufacturing on the Continent the
fact that European distribution patterns were being modernized
after the American pattern.

Other Reasons for Manufacturing in Europe

While favorable markets are necessary and the profit
motive a stimulus, the motivation behind a particular European investment is complex. Given a profit constraint, the
individual factors can vary from case to case. While the
external variables are the same for all, the organizational
situations and the decision-makers' motivations may differ.

The desire for growth or new worlds to conquer is one consideration. After developing a position in the American market after the Depression and World War II, many companies
were ready for new challenges by the mid-1950's. Growth
with a profit constraint seems to be a major goal of executives
in the modern corporation. A firm's position in the "500"
is part of its social standing. The EEC was promised as a
growth area, plus the romance and prestige of being international. One international vice-president was meeting three
times weekly with the corporate president and executive committee on EEC expansion plans. He said their interest was
very high partly because there was more intrigue and adventure

in their European operations than in their domestic operations, where "everyone knows what to do and things pretty much run themselves."

There was an element of bandwagon and "getting in on the ground floor" psychology in American investment in Europe in the late 1950's. The Common Market became the Number One topic in business circles, and it became even fashionable to invest in Europe. A corporation president scarcely dared to face his stockholders without being able to report on the company's moves in the EEC. This was indeed something of a revolution in the orientation of American business.

Activities of organizations like the American Management Association and the Department of Commerce, as well as extensive publicity in the business press about the Common Market, led to a rediscovery of Europe. This publicity and educational effort on behalf of the EEC did much to remove the peculiarity or strangeness of European and international business. This was also true for many European firms (as the MSI study showed), but it was more important for the Americans. They were told, in effect, that there was a new, large market; that it would be like the American market, not only in size but in new consumption patterns and marketing practices; that Americans would have an advantage because of experience in coping with large markets and mass distribution. Reports of the profits of international firms encouraged the Americans further.

This publicity and the sudden popularity of Europe led some companies to overconfidence and a too casual approach. Mistakes were made. Some firms later dropped particular operations because of losses, while others are still clinging tenaciously to their foothold and hoping for eventual profits. While no one likes to talk about such unfavorable experiences, there were several indications of such trials among respondent companies. This was not the predominant picture, however.

The competitive drive is another motivation for local manufacturing. A chemical company executive explained a particular investment by saying, "If we hadn't gone in, _____ (an American competitor) would have." The pattern of their international investments was determined in part by whether they or an American competitor got there first. The market

would usually support just one producer in their line. A consumer goods firm that dominates its market in the United
States complained that its leading U.S. competitor "had the
overseas market to themselves and were using their foreign
profits to compete against us here." Almost as an after-
thought, he added that the European market looked attractive.
A Chrysler executive explained their over $350 million in for-
eign investments since 1958: "We were at least thirty years
behind GM and Ford in overseas development. We were just
trying to close the gap."[7] The journalist claimed that, "Like
David, Chrysler Corporation is out to take on the Goliaths of
the world automotive market."[8]

In some corporations a change of top management pre-
ceded entry into Europe. Preoccupation with the American
(and in one case, the South American), market precluded investment in Europe. With a new president or a change of
some key top executives (usually younger men in), operations
were begun in Europe. This was sort of an international coun-
terpart to the Sewell Avery experience at Montgomery Ward.

Extensive cash balances are often both an encouragement
and a motivation. A president of one respondent firm noted
these cash-flow pressures, saying: "You can't sit on all that
cash. You have to use it or return it to the stockholders." He
was seconded in this by the president of a leading American
brewery: "We are creating cash flow at a faster rate than is
needed domestically and are being pushed to look for other investments."[9] An automotive executive explained: "We've got
plenty of money to invest, and are looking to invest it wherever
there's a possibility to sell cars." An industrial concern said
it built plants abroad to keep capital, labor, and know-how
fully employed, to maintain strength through diversification,
and to keep the competitive spirit sharp.

Geographical diversification can be a further inducement
to European manufacture. A consumer goods firm with a very
narrow product line used this reason in explaining its Common Market investment to its stockholders. However, firms
with broader lines may also find such opportunities attractive.
The demand for diversification is greater than the supply in
the United States because of antitrust regulations.

The reasons for establishment and expansion of manufacturing facilities in Europe are thus varied and complex. The
important fact is that it did occur and continued even after the
upswing in the American economy that began in 1962. As
Gilbert H. Clee, a director of McKinsey, put it: "The fact
that these companies have continued, and in many cases even
increased, the pace of their expansion overseas is evidence
that full scale participation in the world economy has become
part of their long-term strategic planning."[10]

SPECIALIZATION OR CENTRALIZATION OF PRODUCTION IN THE EEC

Location of supply raises the question of Europe versus
America. Once European production has been decided upon,
there is also the question of where in the EEC the plant or
plants should be located. Is one central plant sufficient for
the whole Common Market, or is one needed for each national
market? With the elimination of tariff barriers, one would
expect a trend to centralized production for the whole Common Market. Nontariff factors, including transportation
costs, could counteract this tendency. Since size of establishment seems to be related to productivity,   larger operations would benefit both the firm and the integrated economies.
This is, of course, one reason for integration.

For the firm that already had plants in several countries,
the opening of a common market would suggest specialization
of production between these plants. This would allow internal
economies of scale rather than the shorter, varied production
runs for narrower national markets. (This is also the hope in
the Canadian-United States' automotive common market.)
This specialization would correspond roughly to the international reallocation of production mentioned by the economists.
Scitovsky and Verdoorn were very pessimistic about gains
from this source in Europe, but Liesner and Balassa are
quite optimistic.[11] Balassa says that "integration will make
the exploitation of economies of scale possible for a number
of industries in the European Common Market."[12] Addressing
himself specifically to the question of interplant economies in
a multiplant firm, he speculates that some gains can be made
but that the lack of data prevents prediction.[13]

The experience of the respondent firms can shed some light on the issue. As noted earlier, the twenty-five companies had a total of eighty-eight country production sources by 1965 and the number was increasing. The number of plants is quite a bit higher than that because several firms have more than one plant in certain countries (including licensee operations). It should be noted that the number of plants is somewhat misleading as to the degree of centralization or specialization of production within the EEC. Even in the United States common market, these same firms have an array of plants because of the geographic extent of the market, its economic size, and a varied product line. Thus, their multiplicity of plants in the EEC does not prove that the EEC is an uncommon market, although it suggests something about heterogeneity.

Consumer Nondurables

A few of the manufacturers of consumer nondurables were serving the EEC on the basis of one plant supplying a product to the whole market. Sample products were photographic film, packaged food or confection, and women's foundation garments. The picture was mixed, however, as some firms had certain plants for national production and others for the whole Common Market. For example, a cosmetics firm was producing largely for national markets, but its newest product was produced in France for the whole EEC. Furthermore, the company had located its most recent EEC plant in view of the eventual realization of the Common Market. Thus, its former national orientation was evolving into an EEC approach (in production).

The majority of the manufacturers of nondurables were producing primarily for national markets and in some cases were expanding investment on that basis. They felt that, for them, a common market was many years away. However, some were not only planning but also taking steps toward producing on a Common Market basis. (Distribution was expected to be national for a longer time than production.) For example, a food company, rather new in Europe and operating through acquisitions, expected to take steps toward rationalizing its production as soon as it had made acquisitions in two more Member Countries. An international veteran with about twenty EEC plants was still expanding national plants for national markets. The executive thought it would be at least

ten years before widespread production specialization was
possible for the firm. Nevertheless, the company had
centralized and specialized its research and development laboratories in the EEC and had a three-country affiliate committee studying the centralization of stores and parts.

Another consumer goods company had gone all the way
in rationalizing production for the Common Market. It had
plants on the Continent before World War II and had expanded
greatly during the early 1950's. With the need for further
major plant expansions, the executives finally decided that,
in the long run, a large centralized plant for the EEC would
be more profitable. They calculated savings of $1.5 million
in investment and annual savings in manufacturing costs almost $2 million greater than the increase in distribution costs.
The other national plants are to be phased out, and there will
remain just national marketing agencies. What makes this
the more notable is the fact that their products and packages
are adapted for each national market. Thus, they have rationalized production with nonstandardized products; but the marketing is still handled nationally. For maximum efficiency in the
production of products with different formulas, the plant is
highly automated and computer-controlled. Besides the financial savings, there are expected to be advantages in new product development, quality control, and consolidation of scarce
management talent in manufacturing. This example has been
cited at greater length as it represents an approach that
should be followed by others in the future.

Consumer Durables

The consumer durables companies were operating generally on the basis of a product plant for the whole Common
Market. A tire producer had some plants that were producing largely for national markets, but as the business grew
it expected market-wide integration of these to the extent
allowed by transportation costs. It already had centralized
research and development for Europe at an EEC location.
Another firm had its major plant in England and a smaller
one on the Continent. When England failed to joint the EEC,
the company had to expand greatly its EEC plant and then
added a large assembly operation in another Member Country.
The respondent said the EEC made this both necessary and
possible. In one firm there was a difference of opinion as

to the eventual success of the Common Market. One executive claimed that they placed their plants as if there were no
EEC, but other executives said they were acting on the as-
sumption of a great degree of integration.

An international pioneer in consumer durables had national production in several countries. At the advent of the Rome
Treaty, the firm had hired an extensive study of its European
operations made by a consultant. As a result, it began, in
1958, a program of rationalization that led to product-by-
plant specialization in the EEC. The cheapest model in the
line is now produced in Italy, which also sells to underdeveloped countries. Coincident with this rationalization was
greater standardization of products in the three main lines.
When the firm wanted to expand its line of durables, it bought
an Italian producer with capacity to serve the whole Common
Market area.

Industrial Goods

In the industrial goods field, one would expect pure technological considerations to outweigh national differences in
tastes and habits and permit more of a common market than
with consumer nondurables. This is what has happened.
Over two thirds of the firms selling to the industrial market
are using an EEC-wide or even a Europe-wide approach
in production planning. For example, one chemical producer,
which has put fifteen plants in Europe since 1958, made a
market study for each product and placed each plant where
it had the largest "domestic" market, i.e., EEC or EFTA
(European Free Trade Association). The plant produces a
product for the whole market, but the demand in the individual country is given some attention. For the plants located
in EFTA, the expected EEC common external tariff was not
considered a serious barrier.

Another firm has realized global integration of manufacturing with maximum interchangeability of parts. An
example was given of this integration: "It is possible to take
a transmission from Detroit, an engine from Italy, other
components from England, and build a tractor to prescribed
specification in France. This component mix could be changed
to include other sources." While this is integration on a global basis, the customs union does tend to make the EEC operations
more self-sufficient than would otherwise be the case.

Some industrial marketers are in the planning stage on
specialization, and others still have not given it much thought.
Operating through licensees is a complicating factor. Exclusive agreements in manufacturing might be accompanied
by nonexclusive agreements in distribution. Whereas tariffs
and other barriers had formerly restricted licensees to national markets, now they are selling more across national
borders, creating new problems. One firm was rationalizing
output in its German and Italian plants, but could do nothing
about its French licensee, which was now getting strong throughout the EEC. The licensor could restrict the licensing of new
products but was handcuffed on its established line.

A few industrial marketers are operating primarily on
a national market basis for various special reasons. For
example, some pharmaceutical firms found national regulations strong and diverse enough to warrant national production. One set up a licensee in Italy to mark time till harmonization of drug regulations would enable its EEC production
to be centralized at its wholly owned operation in Belgium.
A manufacturer of packaging materials has twelve plants in
one Member Country and several more in two others. Transportation costs are an important factor restricting the area
served by each plant. The company is, however, operating
primarily on a national market basis because of competitive
and other reasons and has not given serious consideration
to a total Common Market approach.

CONCLUSIONS

European Manufacture Versus
Exports from America

This study is in agreement with various other records
that   show that local production now constitutes the greater
(and increasing) part of European supply by American manufacturers. Not only was this fact reaffirmed, but it was
found that there are many sound reasons why a firm should
be producing in Europe for the European market. Economic
factors are important, especially the formation of the customs union. There are also political inducements; but perhaps most important are the marketing considerations in
serving the rich, competitive Common Market. Customer

service and market information are enhanced by local manufacture. Product policy and distribution become more efficient with on-the-spot operations. Thus, while the government, labor, or other groups may question expansion of
European production, such a policy is generally sound from
the viewpoint of manufacturers who wish for growth and continuing markets in Europe.

Centralization of Production in the EEC

The experience of these firms suggests the generalization that for industrial marketers and consumer durables
manufacturers, rationalization of production in the EEC is
both feasible and desirable. The particular situation of each
firm will govern the possibilities for it, but the potential
should be carefully studied. It seems that those who have had
the most experience and made the most thorough studies have
gone the furthest toward rationalizing production on an EEC
or European basis. Even when locating for the EEC market,
the national market of the plant country should, of course, be
considered.

For consumer nondurables manufacturers, the EEC is
less homogeneous generally; and the individual country markets must be given more attention. However, even here there
seem to be interesting possibilities for production rationalization, as shown especially by the example of the firm that has
gone all the way to one plant for the EEC, although products
are differentiated for specific Member Countries. If one
looks at the similarities rather than the differences and re-
alizes that many elements of the final product (i. e. , ingredients, parts, or package) can be standardized, there should
be room for increased efficiency. Standardization is one area
where many firms are properly directing attention.

NOTES TO CHAPTER 2

1. Emile Benoit, Europe at Sixes and Sevens: The Common Market, The Free Trade Association, and the United
States (New York: Columbia University Press, 1961), p. 186.

2. Booz, Allen & Hamilton, Inc., New Foreign Business Activity of U. S. Firms -- 54 Months -- 1960-64 (New York: Booz, Allen & Hamilton, Inc., 1965), p. 4.

3. "One Chance in a Thousand," German International, VI, 2 (February 28, 1962), 12.

4. Elizabeth Marting (ed.), The European Common Market: New Frontier for American Business (New York: American Management Association, Inc., 1958), p. 64.

5. Samuel Pizer and Frederick Cutler, "Financing and Sales of Foreign Affiliates of U. S. Firms," Survey of Current Business, November, 1965, pp. 14-24.

6. Richard H. Randall, "Size and Nature of European Electronics Markets," Paper presented at Electronic Industries Association International Symposium, Washington, D. C., March 19, 1963. (Mimeographed) 13 pp.

7. "Chrysler Soups Up Foreign Sales," Business Week, February 8, 1964, p. 47.

8. Ibid.

9. "Schlitz Is Planning Foreign Operations," The Wall Street Journal, March 16, 1964, p. 19.

10. "Major U. S. Companies Increase Overseas Investments Faster Than They Do Domestic Assets," International Commerce, LXIX, 48 (December 2, 1963), 38.

11. Bela Balassa, The Theory of Economic Integration (Homewood, Ill.: Richard D. Irwin, Inc., 1961), pp. 49-53.

12. Ibid., p. 136.

13. Ibid., pp. 142-43.

CHAPTER **3** PRODUCT
POLICY

Establishment of local supply is a significant aspect of
corporate adjustment to the Common Market. However, one
of the most important areas in which adjustment is to be expected is product policy. Since it is the product that provides
the reason for the marketer-buyer encounter, adaptation of
product policy should be an essential element of successful
marketing in the EEC. If the product is not suitable, all
other adjustments will be insufficient for marketing success.

The three aspects of product policy to be considered in
this chapter are the physical product itself, the product line,
and product planning and development for the Common Market.

THE PRODUCT FOR THE
COMMON MARKET

In the present context, the product will be considered primarily in its physical features, leaving packaging, warranties,
etc., for later discussion. There are three developments to
be anticipated concerning a product for the Common Market.
First, the new interest and investment in the EEC should lead
to a product adapted for Europe. Since European tastes and
requirements are different from those of America for many
products, there would be greater success in offering a product
tailored for Europe than in offering the American product.
Product adaptation is facilitated by local manufacture.

Secondly, the opening of the Common Market should lead
to greater standardization of products. Improved communications, the activities of EEC or international trade associations,
and the Rome Treaty program for harmonizing national regulations are all influences for standardization. This concept
can have two expressions: the interchangeability of parts of
different manufacturers, or the reduction of product variety
by an individual producer.[1] We are primarily concerned here

with the reduction of product variety, i.e., uniformity of product throughout the EEC versus product modifications for individual Member Countries.

Thirdly, because of rising incomes in the EEC and a decade of relative prosperity, there should be an upgrading in the products offered--products with features similar to those offered in the American market, i.e., larger size, more convenience or luxury or power. The American influence through the G.I., tourists, movies, and exports is strong in Western Europe.

Adaptation

Most of the producers of consumer nondurables have made product adaptations for the EEC in some, if not all, of their products. The only exceptions in the sample were in women's foundation garmets and chewing gum. In the former, the American (and even "Made in U.S.A.") image was an important selling point. In the latter, the product is definitely considered American and owes much of its market to the G.I. influence. While the American producer played down the "Americanness" of the product, local competitors emphasized it, even to the point of labeling their packages in English and using American names--just as French names are used on some American-made perfumes.

About half of these firms had made adaptation in part of their line while retaining the identical American product in the rest. For example, a company selling cosmetics and toiletries saw itself as "an American firm selling American products to a world market"--but it did do some local adaptation. A soft drink company kept its top drink (a cola drink) the same worldwide (cola drinks are also considered "American" in Europe), but adapted its other beverages extensively according to local tastes, color preferences, and national regulations such as per cent of fruit juice required. One food firm started to distribute its U.S. products, but with no success. It then adapted some of its products and came out with some new items for the local market and began to prosper.

Four of the eleven manufacturers of nondurables practiced a rather general across-the-board policy of adaptation to European or even to national markets. Their lines included packaged

foods, home-care items, and home and personal paper products.
All four were supplying the market almost entirely by local
manufacture. Though their European products were of the
same type as those produced in America, modifications were
made in formula, flavor, or texture. Two companies practiced this policy long before the Rome Treaty, but the other two
started product modification when they began local production
in the late 1950's. All agreed that, for them, obtaining of profitable volume required extensive adaptation of product to
local market characteristics.

In the field of consumer durables, there was unanimity
among respondents in modifying products or in making new
ones for the European market. This policy frequently antedated the EEC; but even when it did, the Common Market
usually gave it new impetus, especially with the initiation or
expansion of local manufacture. A tire firm that had been
selling through both export and local manufacture opened another plant in the EEC and then found that it had to change its
line from that previously exported to that country. A refrigerator manufacturer was exporting some American models but
also licensed an Italian firm to make a "European-sized" refrigerator.

With durables there may be pressures from three sources
for product adaptation: technical requirements, such as different electrical voltage and cycles; government regulations,
such as those which affect tire construction or, through taxes,
the horsepower of cars; consumer habits, such as frequent
grocery shopping and customary storage of tall wine bottles
in refrigerators. An example of adaptation of an automatic
washer illustrates some of these pressures and resulting adjustments. Because of the different voltage used in Europe,
a transformer is put into the washer; because Europeans tend
to wear clothes longer before cleaning, the dirt is in deeper --
so housewives like to use boiling water. Therefore, an extra
heater is put on to assure boiling. Because Europeans buy durables for the long haul and fear enamel will chip, a stainless
steel basket was developed for European washers. One appliance manufacturer said: "The most competitive product
to sell in Europe is one incorporating basic American know-
how modified and finished by European designers who know
European requirements."

Among the industrial goods manufacturers, product adaptation is less extensive and different in nature from that of the other product categories. Technological considerations are more important than consumer tastes and habits. Generally, the adaptation in the industrial field consists of tailoring the product to individual customer or industry need, just as in the United States. While economic integration has no logical connection with this type of adaptation, it is notable that the opening of the Common Market has frequently led to an increase in local service staff to seek out new applications and modifications for particular customers and industries. This is true both in the expansion of local manufacturing and in licensee operations. This increase in local service adaptation is found in industries ranging from chemicals to electrical equipment to packaging.

While technical requirements are predominant, there are other factors requiring adaptation by certain industrial concerns. For example, pharmaceutical firms are tightly bound by national regulations that usually require some modification of the basic product as sold in America. Business machines must be adapted to the language or currency of the particular country.

Standardization

The reasons calling for product adaptation to the European market often call for adaptation to individual national markets as well. This means that there is usually a lack of standardization in consumer nondurables in the EEC. All but one of the firms interviewed that had adapted products for Europe had also modified them for particular national markets. One firm had succeeded in attaining standardization in its line of photographic supplies in Europe after a five-year struggle. Before, differences in national demand had prevailed, but now the executives had been able to convince their subsidiaries to standardize. One of the directors noted: "The Common Market is a great persuader."

The other producers of nondurables found standardization progressing rather slowly. While many firms had one leading product that was standard for the whole market, they usually were not optimistic about complete standardization. Some thought another ten years would show great improvement, but

another said: "It won't come in our lifetime." One company
had not even started to standardize because it wanted first to complete its acquisition program in two other Member Countries.
Most, however, had some kind of program and were "going
through the standardization aches," as one put it. One executive, whose firm achieved notable success, said his company
always had had this goal of standardization, but hadn't made
progress till after the Common Market began. This change
was a result of the greater attention to, and control of, its
European business.

There is generally greater EEC standardization of consumer durables than of nondurables. In automobiles, for
example, one producer found the differences between Member
Countries to be no more significant than those between the
States here. One appliance manufacturer found no important
product differences between countries, while another mentioned
only the French preference for front-loading washers versus
the Italian liking for top loaders. The incompatibility of
color TV systems in Europe is a notable exception here.

The progress in standardization of durables results from
the efforts of both manufacturers and international trade associations. Standardization is far from complete, however.
For example, a rubber company executive complained of the
lack of standardization in tires. He said a leading European
company was fighting standardization efforts, feeling that they
would benefit the Americans more. Another durables manufacturer had made great strides toward replacing national by
EEC production, but still had problems in reaching complete
standardization. Its long-standing national organizations were
reluctant to go all the way.

Some observers have said that the Common Market will
exist first in the industrial market. That is true for chemicals, business machines, and many types of equipment. In
these products, the hindrances to standardization are not
national but only in the tailoring of the product or application
to a particular customer or industry need. It is also true
that this situation frequently existed even before the Rome
Treaty.

While standardization has progressed furthest in the industrial market, it is not complete here either. A variety

of reasons hinders its realization. For example, diverse
national regulations are still crucial for drug manufacturers
(although two respondents from this industry were pleased
at the progress made and foresee a common market in drugs
in the 1970's). Organizational reasons prevented standardization for an equipment manufacturer. While its European
products were based on the American models, its old
British and German subsidiaries had gone pretty much on
their own way. The respondent bewailed the fact that "their
products are totally native with very little parts interchangeability."

A manufacturer of farm equipment noted some particularly
nettlesome problems in regard to tractor standardization.
There were at least eight features involved in diverse national regulations and habits: (1) speed requirements, (2) type
of brakes, (3) type of lights, (4) position of lights, (5) turn
signals, (6) hitches, (7) engine horsepower, and (8) type of
fender. (For example, in Germany, a flat fender with handle
was needed so the farm hand could ride on it to the fields.)
He mentioned that a particular model in one plant might have
to meet twelve different "specs" in one day and that a plant
with a capacity of 150,000 units might put out only 100,000
because of the lack of standardization. P. J. Verdoorn suggests that, in explaining productivity differentials between
the United States and Europe, differences in the length of the
production run may be more important than differences in
plant size.[2]

Upgrading or "Americanization" of
Products in the Common Market

In the conferences and publicity about the EEC, there
were frequent suggestions that the new wealthier Europe was
ready for "American type" products. This was one inducement
to American manufacturers to participate in the market. The
experience of the respondents after six years of the Common
Market will shed some light on the "Americanization" question. The term itself was disliked by most respondents, who
preferred expressions such as "modernization" or "rising standard of living." All found that rising incomes were accompanied
by rising sales of their products, including the industrial field
with its derived demand.

Most of the consumer nondurables respondents said they were selling either "American" products or "American quality" products in Europe. The executives said there had been no upgrading; they had sold this type since the beginning. However, the reason some of them had entered Europe in the late 1950's was because they saw a new market growing for their American-type products. Several mentioned that the democratization of consumption and new consumer habits were following the pattern here in America in recent decades. Comparing the transformation which occurred in the American economy from 1920-50 does indeed remind one of what is happening on an accelerated basis in Europe.[3] A cosmetics firm found that its products, which reach a mass market in America, were now penetrating a mass rather than a class market in Europe. Women's magazines and rising income are helping the Prime Minister's wife's maid to look as chic as the lady aristocrat.[4]

While many firms maintained their traditional American-quality products, there were examples of upgrading to follow rising incomes. In paper goods, one respondent noted how Europe was leapfrogging stages of product development to accept the latest product. Europe was never a profitable market for wax paper, but now plastic and aluminum wrap are being accepted. In toilet tissue, the company spent a lot of money trying to introduce the quality that has the largest share in America. This was considered an improvement over older European types, but there was no acceptance. To its surprise, it found greater success with the more luxurious two-ply roll in colors. A food firm was upgrading its starchy staples to fancier products, such as puddings. Rising consumer income made it unnecessary for a chewing gum manufacturer to produce a cheaper product developed to sell at a lower price. This product is now destined for underdeveloped countries.

It is in the area of consumer durables that the most conspicuous product upgrading and market expansion have occurred. Bigger, fancier, more expensive products are being sold by manufacturers of cars, tires, appliances, and flooring and ceiling materials. A respondent noted that there is now a good market for such items as floor polishers and hair dryers in addition to growth in the big-ticket appliances. Automatic transmissions are becoming more common in automobiles,

too. However, some cheaper and smaller cameras not sold
in the United States are still marketed in Europe.

As noted in a Reader's Digest survey:

A fact that stands out clearly in the data is that the buying boom, whether by cause or effect or both, coincides
so closely with the start of the Common Market. By
and large, newer products and 'status' products have
been sought in great numbers for the first time since
the beginning year of the EEC, 1958. Two-thirds of
many such products were acquired initially since 1958.
Three of five Europeans find living conditions better
since the EEC began. [5]

Competitive pressures and increasing consumer sophisti-
cation were other reasons mentioned for product upgrading.
Some American firms used to assume they had product lead-
ership partly because of their American development lead.
Now there is new competitive pressure in Europe as com-
petitors there have new strength and technological efficiency.
An automobile marketer said that many consumers were harder
to please because they were buying a car for the second time.
They knew just what they wanted and had money to pay for it.
"They want both economy and luxury," he complained.

In the industrial market, there is less effect of rising
wealth on upgrading of products. There is a tendency to offer
to all the best product available since technical and cost considerations are most important to industrial customers. This
is especially true in chemicals and pharmaceuticals. However, there are examples of upgrading, or perhaps "Americanization," in industrial goods also. A packaging manufacturer
found that rising income enabled the consumer to pay more for
the product and package. This led to an upgrading in the
industry. Equipment manufacturers noted rising demands for
the more sophisticated machinery that represented the top of
their lines in the United States. An economist with one such
firm said that selling of advanced American equipment and
business machines was leading to an Americanization of the
European approach to business problem solving.

Conclusions on the Product

Adaptation

Some respondents said they found that "whatever is good
for America is good for the rest of the world." This is at best
a general guideline, and (especially in the consumer market)
products are likely to need modification for Europe. Certain
goods enjoy a particular American image that is desirable and
facilitates the sale of the American product. Generally, however, a consumer product will enjoy much greater long-run
penetration if it is modified according to the size and other
characteristics desired by the European market. European
manufacture greatly facilitates this adaptation since the principal concern of the local plant can be its local market, whereas exports are usually a peripheral concern to plants in America.

For industrial goods, there is frequently global product
homogeneity. However, even in the industrial market, there
are many instances where adaptation is necessary (either in
product or application) because of national regulations or customer requirements. If the firm's goals are profit maximization and penetration of the European market, the rule would
seem to be product adaptation, with sale of the pure American product the exception.

Standardization

There is little disagreement as to the desirability of product standardization in Europe, but there is a great diversity
of approaches to attaining it. It is probably realized fully only
in chemicals, although some industrial marketers and durables firms have gone as far as national requirements permit.
What remains is often a task for EEC or international standards
organizations or trade associations, and the industrial concern can participate in these to promote progress. The cooperation of European competitors is necessary in this regard,
since any specifically American influence would be suspect.

Some manufacturers of consumer nondurables have yet
to take their first steps toward standardization. Occasionally,
product diversity has arisen because of a lack of coordination
of different national subsidiaries. Even when there is a more
logical reason, there is often room for progress. It is im-

portant for the manufacturer to study the possibilities in light
of the new situation.   Legitimate national requirements should
continue to be recognized, but some differences will probably
be found no longer necessary.   A program should be established that emphasizes the similarities, starting with parts
or ingredients.   With new products, standardization should be
easier since there are no established national product differences to eliminate.   Where products serve a class rather than
a mass market, economic integration should open larger markets to the same social strata, allowing greater standardization. [6] While the gains to be obtained are a function of the
costs of variety, it is probable that a program of standardization will prove profitable to the manufacturer.   Failure to
act will be more costly in the long run.

Upgrading the Product

The right product for the European market will not necessarily be the most expensive or the highest quality.   Marketing research will aid in determining this product, and the manufacturer will also consider his experience in the American
market.   It is perhaps incorrect, as well as undiplomatic, to
speak of "Americanization" of products.   However, it would
be as foolish for the manufacturer to ignore his American experience as to seek to apply it blindly in Europe.   Rising
wealth and improved communications lead to an "internationalization" and upgrading of demand.   The American company
will want to be a leader in meeting this demand.   For this,
its domestic experience will be an asset.

THE PRODUCT LINE FOR THE
COMMON MARKET

When an American manufacturer is thinking of a product
line for Europe, he is apt to start with his American line.
This is natural; but since the European customer and competitive situation are different, it is unlikely that the right
product line for Europe will be identical to the company's
line in America.   Just as adaptation is usually necessary
for individual products, so it is necessary for the whole product line.   The European product line will probably resemble
the American line since that is where the firm has all its
experience.   However, under the push of the profit motive,

it may include some seemingly improbable changes. As one
respondent noted: "We consider ourselves as businessmen
operating for profit in Europe. We are ready to jump in new
directions when we see good opportunities." One example of
this was Colgate-Palmolive's purchase of a prepared food
manufacturer in France.

In addition to adaptation, there is an adjustment of product line that may come from economic integration. One
effect of customs unions predicted by the economists is an increase of specialization resulting from increased competition
in the larger market. This would imply a narrowing of the
firm's product line and specialization according to comparative advantage on an individual firm level. Adaptation and
contraction or expansion of the product line are the adjustments considered in this section.

Adaptation of the Product Line to Europe

Only two of the eleven manufacturers of nondurables products had the same product line in Europe as in America. All
the others had varying degrees of difference from their U.S.
product lines. Most frequently, the European line was smaller
than the American. The leading products from America were
sold in Europe, but not the full line. Occasionally, there
would be a full line in one or two Member Countries where
the firm was best established, with a more limited line, or
even just one leading product, in another country. A soft drink
maker had only its top product in the French market and was
not even selling in the Belgian market. In France, it had as
bottler the largest firm of its kind in the country. This gave
the American firm excellent French distribution, but restricted its product line because of the French bottler's competing
products.

While a company's goal is typically to have its full line
everywhere, the differing competitive situation and the firm's
own history in each country are major factors limiting and
varying the product line. For example, although margarine
is one of its leading products in America, a food firm has
no margarine in its European line because of the predominant
position of Unilever.

In countries where a company was long established, it
would have its widest product line; but where it was trying
to gain a foothold in another Member Country, it would start
with one or a few of its star performers. Thus, a firm
manufacturing in Europe for almost fifty years decided to enter the German market because of the EEC. Its strategy was
to choose a few of its products with the most demonstrable
points of superiority over similar goods already available
in Germany.

Expansion by acquisition played an important role in the
European product line of many manufacturers. The reasons
for the acquisitions were varied: to gain distribution or
manufacturing facilities, to get a broader line, to make a profitable investment, or to acquire European management and
local knowledge. Whatever the reason, the effect was always
to broaden and diversify the product line as the acquired
firm's products continued in production along with those of
the American company. For example, through the purchase
of a French firm, an American food manufacturer acquired
cake mixes in France, but does not sell them in America.
A firm that lost its trademark rights on one of its toiletries
in one Member Country bought a firm producing related
products there and got some new items as well. Operating
through joint ventures has a similar impact on the product
line as the American partner adds some of his products to
the European partner's existing line.

Marketers of consumer durables had product lines very
similar to their American lines. The European line was
usually less extensive but was expanding in the growing market. Both the products and the product line were adapted to
the needs and opportunities in Europe. (Note the Philco example later in this chapter.) One of the newer firms in the
market began by selling a few of the leading products of each
of its divisions. As it expanded European operations, it was
changing from an industrial to a consumer market emphasis
(most of these companies were selling both industrial goods
and consumer durables). This increasing importance of consumer sales was true for two other companies. They expanded
their appliance lines because Europeans are buying everything
from hair dryers to automatic washers.

The competitive situation affected the product lines of these firms relatively less than the nondurables manufacturers. Here again, the extent of the line varied somewhat by country according to the strength and experience of the firm in that country. Acquisitions played a lesser role here; and when they were made, the acquired product line tended to be much closer to that of the American firm than in the case of nondurables. There were, however, new variables affecting products and product line of the durables manufacturers. An automobile marketer noted four factors influencing its line for the Common Market and for individual Member Countries: (1) per capita income, (2) regulations on installment credit, (3) taxes based on the car's horsepower, (4) the price of gasoline. The first two would apply to other durables also.

In industrial goods, there is the closest congruence between American and European product lines. However, except for some equipment manufacturers, the European line is quite a bit narrower than the American. In selling to the industrial market the product line quite naturally depends on the industrial structure in Europe--and in the individual countries. This generally leads to modification of the American line. The other major variable causing adaptation of product line is competition. This is a greater concern to industrial marketers than to the others. Excess capacity has arisen in many fields, and European technology has come up to date more here than in the consumer market, where marketing know-how is relatively more important.

Some examples will illustrate the problem of product line adaptation in the industrial market. A farm equipment manufacturer had its full line in the Common Market area; but in particular countries its line varied according to the agricultural development of the country, its own production there, and competition. It dared not be too aggressive in Italy for fear of stirring up powerful Fiat. Three chemical producers had lines that varied according to the European industrial structure but that were in all cases narrower than in America, primarily because of tough competition. All were tending toward specialty items, where they had some particular edge. As one said: "Europeans now have production capacity in standard items. We are limiting ourselves to products in which we have a unique raw material or technical position. We would rather have 60 per cent of a small but profitable market than 5 per cent of a large cut-throat market."

Pharmaceutical firms have general adaptation problems
plus a few special difficulties. One firm was relatively small
in the Common Market, but it was in antibiotics there and
not in America because of different competitive opportunities.
Another had 600 items in its American line, fifty in the United
Kingdom, and about twenty in Belgium, its largest EEC operation. Not only was competition a factor, but also the question
of registration and reimbursement by government socialized
medicine boards. The international vice-president said:
"One advantage of starting later in Europe than here was that
the international division could pick and choose products according to the market situation. We had no vested interest
in particular products." The chaotic patent situation also
bothered drug manufacturers, but both firms felt progress
was being made toward a uniform EEC patent. While internal
tariffs are no longer a problem, the Six have moved very
slowly in removing nontariff barriers in the drug trade.

Expansion of the Product Line
in the Common Market

The increased competition in the customs union should
lead to an increase of specialization in production. This
would imply a narrowing of a firm's product line[7]--or at
least specialization by plant in a multiplant firm. (The latter topic has been discussed in the chapter on location of
supply.)

The narrowing of a firm's product line after economic
integration would result from two forces. The most profitable products, which could only be sold in the national market
before, can now be sold throughout the customs union. A
firm would want to expand production and specialize on these
products where it has the greatest comparative advantage.
Conversely, the broad line, which a firm was selling in
the protected national market before integration, may find
new competition encroaching on the sales of the weaker products. A firm would want to drop these products where it
has a competitive disadvantage.

Competition has affected the European product lines of
American manufacturers in Europe, but it is not always the
increased competition resulting from economic integration
but often preexisting national competition. The prudent manu-

facturer looks at the competition before entering the European
market. He also looks at national competition before entering a national market. In each case, he will adjust his product
lines to the realities of the situation so as to be entering from
a position of strength. Both consumer and industrial goods
firms tend to limit their European or national line to those
products that have the greatest edge over those already in
the market. Examples of such adaptation have been cited
above.

Increased competition seemed to have a rather small impact on narrowing the American firm's product line in Europe.
A food company did feel it was vulnerable on some prepared
food items. These were not its strongest products, and new
competition was a real threat. Suprisingly enough, the main
new competitor was another American firm that dominates
this particular market in the United States. Chemical firms
mentioned losing standard items ("me too" products) to European producers and concentrating now on specialties. A rubber company had to drop one product, but this was because
it was from its English plant. Competition was able to shut
out a non-EEC source.

Rather than a narrowing, however, expansion of European
product lines was the rule. Twenty-four of the firms had expanded their lines since 1958, and one had the same line as
before. There were a number of reasons for this expansion,
many of which do not contradict the idea of increasing specialization implied by integration.

One of the major reasons for expansion of product line by
American companies was the initiation or expansion of local
manufacturing. This permits European sale of many goods
not economical to export from America. The new facilities
are generally multiproduct plants and enable the American
manufacturer to broaden his line in Europe. A related reason is the new interest by Americans in the now more profitable European market. They want to sell more there, and
that usually means new products in addition to the existing
European line. Another result of this increased interest is
the greater attention and effort put into European operations.
Not only is local manufacturing expanded, but sales and
marketing efforts are intensified. New distribution agreements are made, promotional expenses raised, and European

sales and service personnel multiplied. With all this new
skill and effort available, the American firm finds it can sell
more products than the limited line   that perhaps sold itself before. The combination of local manufacturing and increased sales and service efforts permit much more local
adaptation of product or application. This, in turn, means
that more products are now suitable for the European market,
hence a broader line.

Rising income has promoted broader lines. It is easier
to expand a product line in boom conditions, and these conditions also entice a firm to try for greater profits. With
more money and a certain accumulation of goods, consumers
demand more variety. This is true in both food products and
durables. A buyers' market forces the producer to meet this
demand. Competitive pressure often forces extension of product line. This was mentioned especially by marketers of consumer durables. This was partly an active policy of market
segmentation and partly a defensive strategy to meet competitors throughout the line. Volkswagen had to add the "1500"
model to its traditional "1200." General Motors' Opel now
has a line to compete with both VW and Mercedes. [8] A soft
drink firm came out with a full line of fruit flavors to meet
competition across the line.

New-product development was another important factor
in expanding product lines. As the company develops new
products in America or Europe, these are added to the line
and usually strengthen its competitive position. Through ac-
questions, many have expanded their European lines. Because of the acquired lines, several firms are selling products in Europe that they don't have in America. The frequent
company goal of a full line in each country operation exerts
pressure for expansion. One firm even used the managers of
acquired companies as sort of good-will ambassadors to travel
to other countries to investigate possibilities of adding their
products. Finally, aggressive profit-seeking pushed some
firms into lines that they were not selling in America but
that they were in a favorable position to present in Europe.
Thus, a food firm was licensee for an American baby food
manufacturer and two other American specialty food producers. It felt Europe was ready for mass marketing of these
items; and it had the facilities and experience for producing
and distributing them, whereas the firms selling them in
America couldn't handle the business in Europe by themselves.

The net effect of all these influences was an expanded, rather than a contracted, product line. Companies felt they were in a stronger competitive position with a wider line. The reasons were not generally related to costs of production, as in the specialization argument, but were marketing reasons and dynamic factors in a situation not characterized by theoretically pure competition.

Philco is an example of some of the product-line adjustments and advantages available to an American multinational manufacturer competing in Europe. [9] Philco's European washing machine line includes two models from Britain, two of Italian design, and a wringer model from the United States. Its refrigerator line counts seventeen models, seven designed in Italy plus ten from the United States.

This approach gives the multinational firm several advantages. A wide product line is available without sacrificing economies of scale because several production sources are used. Greater diversity and adaptation are possible than when relying only on national or EEC sources of supply. The company is able to sell in all price ranges and to all market segments on a profitable basis. Generally, these advantages derive from the possibility of specializing on a larger-than-EEC basis. Ability to do this depends, of course, on the tariff and transportation costs for the goods involved.

Conclusions on the Product Line

For successful marketing, the American manufacturer should adapt his product line for Europe. It will resemble his American line but be modified according to the differing market opportunities and competitive possibilities. The European line will probably be narrower. Each product should be analyzed for the particular niche it may find there. This will result in a pruning away of many American products that have no market justification in Europe, but that may have a vested interest or traditional role in the firm's American operations. On the other hand, the new, advanced products are likely to be appropriate in modern Europe. A European marketing consultant noted the following characteristics of the products for "tomorrow" in Europe: First, they should be ready-made or ready to cook; second, they should be easy to handle, as "no return" bottles; third, they should be "continental style", i.e., continent wide; fourth, they should be finer and more colorful; fifth, there will be faster fashion changes. [10]

The products that make up the European line will be characterized by their competitive superiority, whereas the "me too" products will be left at home. This superiority may be technological or may result from a better adaptation to consumer wants. In either case, a company can enter from a position of strength with such a line, and this represents a form of specialization according to comparative advantage. Special opportunities in Europe may draw a firm into lines different from its American operation. This should be done with caution, however, as a company's competitive edge presumably arises from its American marketing and technical experience. Getting away from this might leave a firm without a maintainable advantage. Of course, long experience in Europe gives a firm another advantage that might give it more freedom in its product line. Some veterans in Europe gave their local subsidiaries wide authority to select the products for the line in their country.

PRODUCT PLANNING AND DEVELOPMENT

Adaptation of product and product line implies special attention to European requirements. With the greater attention given to the EEC, and especially with local production, there should be much greater care given to product planning for the Common Market. There should be more product research in Europe and perhaps a new product laboratory there, or else greater attention to European needs in the domestic product-planning program. Changing consumer preferences in Europe and the increasingly competitive market reinforce the need for this.

All the firms do most of their basic product research in America. This is a function of historical development, size of market and staff, and the desire for specialization. Almost all give special attention to European product needs but in varying degrees. There are four ways in which this is done (and a firm may utilize more than one method): Foreign requirements may be fed into United States product planning,

acquired companies may continue their own programs, the
licensees or joint-venture partner may do it, or the American company may have its own laboratories in Europe.

European Product Requirements Fed into United States Product Planning

To accomplish this, there are two conditions to meet:
The local requirements must be determined, and they must
be communicated. In consumer goods, a formal type of
marketing research is often necessary to determine desired
product quality. Some of the larger, more experienced firms
will do their own research, while firms newer in the market tend to hire an American or European agency. Distributors
or licensees can be helpful, too, especially if the line is relatively important to them. Subsidiary personnel are an
important information source, and they are usually nationals.
Sales and service staffs in Europe are often the major prod-
uct-idea source for firms selling to the industrial market.
They are usually technical people and work closely with customers, so there is direct feedback. One equipment manufacturer found trade fairs useful also.

Communication is apparently no serious problem today.
Besides the formal communications, there are frequent trips
by American marketing and product specialists to Europe
and by their counterparts from Europe to America. Some of
the larger companies always have one or more Europeans
here in America, and one had annual meetings of its product-planning people from all subsidiaries. One respondent,
a marketing director, had just returned from two weeks in
Europe. His first task on returning was to meet with the
product-design department to discuss European reaction to
the new American product samples he had taken there. Perhaps too obvious to mention is the time requirement. European product needs must be communicated to the United
States product-planning activity at an early enough stage to
be economically incorporated into the development of the
product.

Acquisitions, Licensing, and Joint Ventures

For firms more recently in the market by acquisition or
those with the less complete commitment of licensing or joint

venture, much of the product development and adaptation was
done by the European firm. A food firm introduced its leading United States products into the lines of the acquired companies, which continued their own product-development program.
The American company said it lacked qualified personnel and
experience and thus could not take stronger control at present. A licensee may be an important source of ideas and
facilities for product adaptation and development. That is one
reason why licensing agreements can be hard to terminate.
The licensee may have reached the "take-off" stage and be a
potentially serious competitor. In joint ventures, the European partner may have long experience in the market and an
ongoing program of product development. The American
partner is generally happy to have this continue and will contribute technical and marketing help for an enhanced program.
In one case, however, a paper goods company joined with a
processor with few finished goods. Here product development was one of the specific American contributions. Much
depends, obviously, on the nature of the European partner.

European Laboratories

Many of the firms had one or more European laboratories.
This was true in both consumer and industrial goods. These
laboratories were of various sizes and were put to diverse
uses. Some were used only for testing and quality control.
However, one chemical firm considered its Swiss laboratory
as its "eyes and ears" in Europe because "they're not behind
us in R and D now." Another agreed on European research
progress but saw no value in a laboratory there--"The best
way to learn about competitors is to sell against them."
Some noted that there was "more research for a dollar"
in Europe.

A few firms had European laboratories that were charged
with product development for Europe. In these cases, the
basic research was done in the United States, but the develop-
mental work in Europe. A manufacturer of home-care products had a professional staff of sixty in its new London center
and 200 in the United States. The American staff was larger
primarily because it did the basic research that formed the
basis of the applied work in London. A rubber company had
a similar arrangement. Design was a major local activity
for an automobile firm.

Other firms had European laboratories or product-development departments with both local and international responsibilities. Some companies had product-development departments in each producing subsidiary. Duplication was avoided in one firm by requiring any project of more than $4,000 to be approved in the United States. This assured continual review of major efforts. Another coordinated work through an annual meeting of all its product-development directors in which tasks were assigned for the coming year. Any national representative would be given approval for any project for which a sufficient national or international market could be foreseen. A food firm had similar international specialization in its development work. It coordinated tasks through a World Director of Research. It was also building a large research facility on the East Coast that was to be 80 per cent devoted to international product development.

The formation of the Common Market was an important influence in this process of decentralization of product development. Some respondents said it was the principal reason. Even where the basic product development was carried on in America, there as a significant increase in product adaptation in Europe--or localized application in the case of some industrial products. A drug firm was still doing its product adaptation in the United States but said the next project in the international division was to decentralize this activity to the EEC.

There is an extra gain from doing research in Europe besides product ideas and potential cost savings. That is the public relations gain. Because of their worries about the "technology gap," Europeans will look more hospitably on an American manufacturer who does research in Europe in addition to production and marketing.

New Product Ideas from Europe

With increased research activity and personnel in Europe, one would expect some new product ideas to cross the Atlantic westward. Multiplying the centers of product development should multiply the ideas also.[11] This can be a fringe benefit from European operations. Of course, for this to occur there must be good communication between European and American operations and a receptive environment on the

American side. If these exist, however, there is no reason
why valuable product ideas should not originate in Europe,
not only for Euopean markets but even for the American. As
one respondent said: "We have no monopoly on brains."
In some cases, one of the responsibilities of local managers
was to get new product ideas or adaptations.

Most of the firms had received some benefits along this
line. (One firm, however, had no success here in spite of
many efforts--including an employee suggestions box.) A
few examples may be mentioned in the area of consumer nondurables. Some firms had found new food items or paper products from their European operations. One had gotten new
packaging ideas and another cost-cutting processes from
Europe.

Consumer durables producers mentioned the "stud" tire
for driving on ice, disc brakes, and the compact car. It
was the European division of one company that came up with
the idea of a full appliance line for their own retail outlets.
This idea was being carried over to United States operations.

This benefit seemed to be most important to manufacturers
of industrial goods. There are two principal reasons for this.
These firms generally had better European resources for getting ideas, i.e., larger research staffs and/or more sales-
service personnel. Furthermore, the fact that technology is
the major consideration in the industrial market means that
there is greater product carry-over from the European to the
American market than is the case with consumer goods.

A few examples will be noted from the industrial market.
Some chemical companies were licensees or joint partners
of European firms in America. Another had developed a
special plastic application for Volkswagen and was going to
market it in the United States. It had found several such
new applications and said,"Europe is often ahead of us on
this score." A farm equipment firm came up with a special
narrow tractor that had a market outside of Europe. An
equipment manufacturer found no new products for the
United States, "but each division in Europe develops products for its own market." A packaging firm had a research
man in Europe full time to observe developments. It had
several licensing agreements in America from European

firms. A well-publicized and related example is the role of
I.B.M.'s European subsidiaries in the design and program-
ming for its System 360.[12]

While profits are the major reason for undertaking European operations, it seems the Old World will have still further
contributions to make to the New World. Italian opera and
French wine were part of the earlier contribution; Italian style
clothing and French engineering logic in a modern computer
are part of the new.

NOTES TO CHAPTER 3

1. Bela Balassa, The Theory of Economic Integration (Homewood,
Ill.: Richard D. Irwin, Inc., 1961), p. 136.

2. Ibid., p. 137.

3. Frederick Lewis Allen, The Big Change: America
Transforms Itself, 1900-1950, (New York: Harper & Brothers,
1952), pp. 109-233.

4. "Si Elle Lit, Elle Lit Elle," Time, May 22, 1964,
p. 69.

5. John F. Maloney, "First Marketing Survey of the
Common Market and Britain," International Advertiser, IV,
8 (August, 1963), 14. The earlier American experience is
reported by Allen, op. cit., p. 213.

6. Balassa, op. cit., p. 37.

7. Balassa, Ibid., p. 127.

8. "G.M. v. Everybody," Time, March 13, 1964, p. 98.

9. "To Succeed in Europe, Philco Goes European," Business Week, October 2, 1965, pp. 132-41.

10. Bertil Neuman, "Europe's Consumer Goods Requirements," Producing for European Markets (London: British
Productivity Council, 1961), p. 9.

11.   John Jewkes, David Sawers, and Richard Stillerman, The Sources of Invention (New York: St. Martin's Press, 1959), pp. 197-260.

12.   T. A. Wise, "I.B.M.'s $5,000,000,000 Gamble," Fortune, September, 1966, pp. 118ff.

CHAPTER **4** PROMOTION

In this discussion, "promotion" will be used broadly to
include such elements of marketing practice as advertising,
brands and trademarks, packaging and labeling, warranties
and service policies, and personal selling. While these are
different means of promotion, there are two developments
one would expect to affect all of them. First, there should
be an intensified use of the various promotional tools by
American companies in the EEC. Their increased interest
in the European market suggests greater promotion to reach
their new goals. Furthermore, the new competition in the
Common Market would force a rise in the use of such competitive weapons to maintain or expand market share. Secondly, there should be increased standardization in the promotional approach throughout the EEC. Contributing to this
growing uniformity are the removal of barriers between
Member Countries, improved communications, and the harmonizing of diverse national regulations.

ADVERTISING

Increase

In the decade of the 1950's, Gross National Product in
Europe rose about 4 per cent annually, whereas advertising
outlays rose from 8-10 per cent yearly.[1] One would expect
American manufacturers to be leaders in increasing the use
of advertising because of their new interest and investment
in Europe and their more aggressive marketing approach.
The task of advertising is to gain recognition, acceptance,
and, hopefully, preference for the advertiser's product.
American manufacturers going into Europe generally have
to work vigorously to attain some semblance of the stature
and recognition they enjoy in the American market. The
famous nonadvertiser, The Hershey Company, found it
needed advertising to break into the Canadian market.

Of the twenty-two respondent firms who used advertising in Europe, all had increased it absolutely and half had
also increased it relative to sales since 1957. Even for those

59

who did not have a relative increase, booming sales usually meant a great absolute rise in advertising outlays. Of course, in the industrial market, personal selling was the major promotional tool; and two firms were not advertising at all. One noted, however, that though it was not advertising heavily in Europe because of various restrictions, relatively greater reliance was placed on advertising there than in America because of inadequate personal selling. Sometimes in Germany, its tractors were sold through cooperatives with eight or nine other models--and no salesmanship.

There are several factors that tend to limit advertising outlays in Europe: diverse national restrictions on advertising, differing industry and consumer reaction to it, the lack of market-wide media, and the lack of reliable data on circulation. Several consumer marketers mentioned that if commercial TV became available throughout the Common Market, there would be a big rise in their advertising outlays. The need to obtain distribution before beginning advertising was noted by some. For example, one consumer marketer carried forward an expensive advertising campaign in Italy and lost money because it hadn't obtained sufficient distribution. Because of this experience, a new rule was established that "No advertising may be undertaken without at least fifty per cent distribution." In-store promotion is the first step now.

Though there are these limits to the use of advertising, there seems to be great potential for it. A food company that   advertises heavily in the United States does none in the EEC. It operates through well-established European firms acquired in the late 1950's and says that "advertising is not used in this industry in Europe." However, this attitude seems to be partly a result of its newness in the market and its relatively passive approach there. This same firm successfully broke industry tradition in England. The Proctor and Gamble experience seems to argue for more advertising also. According to Mr. Henkel, president of the leading German detergent firm:

> The Americans try to win the market most of all
> by intensive advertising campaigns. It has been es-
> timated that the American firms spend at least twice
> as much money on advertising as the European detergent

industry has been accustomed to spend. According to
official statistics, Proctor and Gamble spent an estimated twenty-two million D-marks in one year for the
promotion of just one detergent: Tide. We may say
that they 'bought' a market share of approximately 15
per cent in this manner. [2]

After beginning manufacture in Marseille in 1955, Proctor
and Gamble was second in the French detergent industry by
1963. [3] American companies with advertisable products should
be ready to advertise in Europe, even if national competitors
do not. They may be missing a competitive advantage by not
advertising. Of course, the campaign must be suited to the
local market.

Reasons for Increase in Advertising

There was a variety of reasons given by those who had an
increase in advertising outlays relative to sales. Those who
were serving the EEC only by export in 1957 usually had minimal promotion programs then. One company set up local
production and had increased its total promotional program
"over one hundred fold since 1957. We were only order takers
then. " It now has twelve European plants and spends several
million dollars annually on its over-all promotion. This happened on a smaller scale with several others. Local manufacturing and the new interest in Europe led to a more agressive approach.

The difficulty of entering new markets was another factor.
One firm found that its advertising per cent of sales was lower
in countries where it was well established than in the United
States. However, the per cent was much higher in Member
Countries it had just entered. Another consumer marketer
operating through export used a flat 9 per cent of sales for
promotion, just as in the United States. However, to break
into the German and French markets in 1957-1958, it had an
exceptionally high expenditure.

New-product introduction requires a rise in advertising
expense. A food company noted that on its established line
advertising was relatively lower than in the United States
because of media and other restrictions. However, because
it had introduced many new items in Europe in recent years,

its total advertising outlays were relatively higher there. As noted in Chapter 3, new-product introduction is a frequent occurrence for American firms in the EEC.

New competition was a further important element requiring an increase in advertising expense. One firm had enjoyed a relative monopoly for several years. Now there was a number of competitors, and the original firm was forced to increase its advertising effort to maintain its share of the growing market. A soft drink company noted the new competition and said "the serious problem now is in keeping space in the retail outlet. The retailer has to be convinced that you're preselling the product."

Standardization

Along with rising outlays there should be increasing standardization of advertising in the Common Market. The reduction of barriers to trade, improved communications, and the presence of American manufacturers and advertising agencies are all forces encouraging greater standardization. There are also groups of European agencies and media banding together, often on a Common Market-wide basis. There are group efforts at elimination of national differences in advertising legislation and practice.

Erik Elinder, a Swedish advertising executive, has argued forcefully for an international approach to advertising and against those who claim that each campaign must be prepared in detail by those in the market concerned.[4] He said that this was occurring by itself over time and that positive steps should be taken to accelerate the process for more efficient advertising. This would please American marketers, who are used to a uniform domestic approach and would like its tidiness, ease of control, and economy. However, it must be kept in mind that the most economical advertising is that which does the best job for the money--not necessarily that which costs least. Realities in the market should weigh heavier than the abstract idea.

Much has been written about this on both sides of the Atlantic and on both sides of the question. There is frequently some bias according to the agency or organization to which the writer belongs. The experience of the respondent firms

can clarify the issue somewhat. Since most of the companies
were selling throughout the EEC, the question was relevant to
them.

Reasons for Continuing Diversity

Most of the companies had promotional programs that
still varied on a national basis in the EEC. These differences
were over and above the expected language variation. This
national variation was less prominent for industrial marketers,
who also did less advertising. There were many causes of
this lack of a standardized EEC promotional program. Firms
who had been long in the market had subsidiaries operating
on a national basis before the EEC. Inertia often combined
with local interest to hinder a change in approach.

Firms operating through acquisitions or joint ventures
were often newer in the market and frequently left much of
the promotional program to the acquired firm or partner.
Older national approaches would thus tend to continue. Licensors had limited control over their licensees' advertising,
which was still primarily national in character and coverage.
The fact that most companies used different agencies in each
Member Country contributed to diversity of approach. This
diversity of agency utilization was partly accidental -- i.e.,
the choice was left to the subsidiary or partner in each country
-- and partly deliberate. One company, which leads its
field in Europe, makes a point of choosing agencies that are
local both in location and nationality, i.e., not American.
The respondent said that this was part of being a "good local
citizen." Where subsidiaries are profit centers, they need
a lot of authority over a matter as important as promotion.
Encouragement of local initiative was another reason for
giving subsidiaries authority in this area. One executive
claimed, "We get the best local effort if they're responsible. The benefits of standardization would be more than
outweighed by the loss in local initiative."

Differing characteristics of national markets, or of the
firm's position in these markets, were of primary importance in influencing companies to take a national approach.
These reasons are external to the firm,whereas those discussed above are generally internal influences. The language
is the first, though not the major, distinction between national

markets.   Differing national laws regulating advertising are
a second problem.   Third, media coverage and availability
differ from one country to another.   Fourth, consumer tastes
and habits are still quite heterogeneous in the EEC.   Fifth,
the firms' competitive situations often vary greatly from
country to country.   Sixth, the firms' product lines frequently
differ from one Member Country to another.

Progress Toward Standardization

There are, then, numerous and sometimes weighty reasons
for a national promotional approach.   That is only part of the
picture, however.   Some of the firms were using quite a uniform approach to the EEC market.   Several industrial marketers were switching from a product to an industry approach,
and this was the same in all Member Countries.   One said
that this approach gave it more efficient use of its trade-jour-
nal advertising.   This was placed locally by a correspondent
of the New York agency--after translation but with minimal
local adaptation.   Both the illustration and the theme were
generally the same.   A soft drink marketer said "languages
differ; people don't. " The Reader's Digest management tended
to subscribe to the theory of universality with good success.
A manager of the International Edition said: "The Digest has
a lot of evidence to support the theory of universality, but
not always, and therefore everything is tested and retested
in advance. "[5]

Probably because of such evidence and the control and
economy advantages of standardization, well over half of the
firms had taken steps to increase the uniformity in their
Common Market advertising programs. In line with their new
interest in Europe, they were spending more money and pay-
ing greater attention to promotional programs there.   For
one thing, this meant that there was a more conscious attempt
to follow the approach used in America.   Several mentioned
that they were following their American promotional programs as far as it was possible in Europe.   Since a lot of
experience, effort, and money had gone into these, it was
felt that they should also have something of value for the
Continent.   Said one, in referring to "American" methods:
"They work for us everywhere when they're modified to reflect local differences. "

Most firms made sure that American materials and experience were available to European operations. One had a sales promotion staff of thirty in its international office in New York, and part of its job was to "get the cream of U.S. ideas in advertising and promotion" to send to its European operations. Even Italians were promised a "Ford in your future. "[6]

Some industrial marketers had achieved more uniformity by a new approach. They had changed from product promotion to promotion to an industry, stressing what their firms (rather than one of their particular products) could do for that industry. This led to a corporate-image type of advertising that was deliberately quite uniform all over. Some were striving for a Europe-wide corporate recognition such as they enjoy in the United States, while others were trying to build a uniform worldwide image. One said: "Building a corporate image is about all you can do. The media and supply situation make it difficult to reach a particular market at a particular time for more direct advertising. "

The increased availability and use of American advertising agencies in Europe also aided uniformity. A few companies deliberately chose American agencies in Europe, either because they were with them in the United States or because they could get the same agency in each European country. One international pioneer had increased its employment of a leading American agency in Europe because it was needed for global campaign coordination of a new-product introduction. The respondent noted: "They have some weak links in their chain but they're improving them under client pressure. " There was some disagreement, however, about using American agencies exclusively in Europe. One company that did complained of weak spots and said: Logic demands a European agency. " Another said: "They don't coordinate anything. "

Another influence for greater standardization was the increase in active coordination and control of promotion by the American manufacturers. Usually as part of reorganization for international business, many companies added executives who are responsible for European or international advertising control. Several firms had regional advertising directors in Europe--in London or one of several cities on the Continent. This was in addition to the promotional personnel in each subsidiary. One veteran internationalist had just hired an advertising coordinator for its European division in New York. It had tried coordinating in various ways but had no success till it hired a qualified specialist. Another corporation also had an advertising director for international business. The respondent explained: "We used to just follow agency advice but now we do our own thinking first and use our dollars more effectively." The new, or newly recognized, need for global coordination means more centralized control of advertising and greater uniformity.

This experience of one firm is rather typical. It saw each country subsidiary going a different direction. Now each one draws up a promotional plan and submits it long before the year begins. It is reviewed to see if it meets the common denominators of the marketing program. The company has a staff in New York for international promotion--with a major section for Europe. For new-product introduction, "We provide the basic information and suggest how it should be presented. Sometimes, we persuade with a sledge hammer, but with profit centers, a compromise is reached. "

The assignment of responsible specialists contributes to standardization in several ways. In proving himself as a "new broom," the new executive tries in many ways to improve and bring new order to the old situation. There is more effective interchange of ideas and experience of the company in many countries. As one said, "We coordinate to be sure that our successes in one place are used or available elsewhere--and that our failures aren't repeated. That's the value of multinational experience. "

There is now more planning on a global or regional basis as opposed to the strictly national approach that usually prevailed before. One firm was trying for a "Unilever or Nestle image," which it felt was European or international without having the disadvantage of being associated with a particular country. Some found that national differences were less important than they had thought. As one respondent explained: "We were told we must follow

local tastes, but we found that good taste is good anywhere."
This was from a European national with one company. However, whereas one company found that the Common Market
was a "great persuader" in helping to bring greater uniformity,
another executive said: "Our European managers say we can't
go any faster along this line. I think they're right. The national differences are still too important for us."

Conclusions on Advertising Adjustment

The first and most important step is a reassessment of
promotional strategy for the Common Market. A careful study
of all the relevant competitive and market factors, the progress of integration and harmonization of laws, the firm's
particular situation, and the experience of others will give
the best guidance as to the desirable strategy for the individual company. Rather than a drift toward standardization,
there should be a positive program for eliminating duplication and nonessential differences, and harmonizing what can
be harmonized from the standpoint of the market. Legitimate
national differences (as opposed to those arising merely from
tradition or vested interest) must continue to be considered.
Care must be taken to have the agreement of subsidiaries
on changes in the promotional program. This will help to
assure their cooperation and avoid the stifling of local initiative and enthusiasm. Of course, standardization should
not be obtained at the price of mediocrity or lifeless promotion.

When the firm has made an adequate study of the new
European environment, it will be able to answer questions
(such as the degree of standardization, or centralization
versus decentralization of advertising control) based on a
knowledge of its own situation rather than on a theoretical
precept or just copying the experience of others. Furthermore, the experience gained in Europe should be invaluable
to the firm as it expands the internationalization or global-
ization of its promotional program. An advertising director
with one firm noted that the Common Market was more like
the United States and, therefore, the company's advertising
was first being standardized there. However, the same approach would be followed in other areas later.

BRANDING

For the present discussion, a brand is defined as any letter, word, name, or symbol adopted by a manufacturer to identify his products. [7]

While the basis of rights to brands differs in Europe (priority of registration in Europe versus priority in use in America), the discussion will be confined to the promotional aspects of branding--and changes in American practice resulting from the Common Market. It should be noted, however, that problems do arise because of the European system of giving rights to brand names.

Two major trends can be expected in American branding practice in the EEC: standardization and adaptation to Europe. The removal of national trade barriers and the development of the Common Market should mean increasingly standardized brands and trademarks by American manufacturers. This would tie in with a market-wide advertising approach. One would also expect brands to be more adapted to the European market in accord with the new emphasis by American marketers there. Both products and brands can be more easily Europeanized with local manufacture--and probably should be for a greater market penetration.

Adaptation to Europe

As to adaptation of brands, the situation differs between industrial goods and consumer goods companies. There is generally little adaptation in the industrial market but much in the consumer market.

For industrial marketers, brand is generally less important than in the consumer field. There is more buying by specification than by brand name in industry. Therefore, it isn't surprising that most companies selling to the industrial market use the same brands in Europe as in America. Often the company name (which acts as a family brand) is more important than the name on a particular product. However, there were a few instances where industrial goods companies did have different brand names in Europe. Two examples will illustrate how this can arise. One firm used

United States names where possible, but in a few cases it
was unable to buy a name from someone who had previously
registered it in a Member Country. An equipment manufacturer used the United States brands globally, but there
was one exception in Germany. After World War I the
American company had bought a large German firm to obtain its production facilities and name and good will. This
gave the American firm dual operations in Germany and a
much larger market share. The German brand has continued
till the present, but now is being phased out and replaced by
the American. Expanding business outside of Germany is the
reason for this change.

In selling to European consumers, American manufacturers have adapted brand names rather extensively. About
two thirds of the consumer goods firms used different brand
names in Europe than in America, although many had one
or more products with the same name. In this latter case,
the product was usually identical also. Where only one or two
of the firm's products had the American brand name, it was
frequently its leading items that had established a market
by export and could continue with that name. Many new products, added perhaps with local manufacture, had no good will
established and were given European or national names.

There was usually a desire to use the American brands
across the product line; but in the absence of established
good will or because of registration problems, the bad connotation, or lack of pronounceability of the name in Europe,
a new brand name was better for the market. Where the
American brand was not known in the market, there was nothing to lose by dropping it and probably much to gain by getting a new one more attractive to European consumers. A
possible exception is when the product gains from its American image, as was claimed for women's foundation garments.

One respondent said that the rise of the Common Market
had encouraged his firm to use market research to find appropriate brand names for Europe. They had come up with
a particularly suitable European name for their line of tires.
One company had long practiced a policy of adaptation and
had up to six different European names for some of its leading home-care products. The company name was a link between them. Some firms newer in the market and working

through acquisitions and joint ventures kept the established consumer franchise of the acquired brand names and products. Respondents of several companies whose brands are household words in America said: "Our name doesn't mean anything in Europe." Even automobile manufacturers have adapted both names and products, e. g. , Ford's Taunus and General Motors' Opel.

Brand adaptation may also be forced on the firm. If the American name has a bad connotation in some countries, a new brand must be chosen. This was true for a soft drink and a personal product of a paper goods firm. Prior registration by another may cost the firm its brand in a market. For example, a food company executive noted that easy registration in Germany led some profiteers to take advantage of the situation by registering names that large companies might want to use later. An automobile manufacturer said the name of its newest sports model was already registered by someone in Germany. The firm could not sell the car or even display it there by that name.

Standardization

All of the forces leading to increased uniformity of products and advertising in Europe affect branding also. The omnipresent European marketer, Unilever, is moving toward standardization because of European integration. It "expects to reshape marketing policies toward more coordination and an increasing use of identical brand names, packages, and advertising themes."[8] A voluntary chain organization has started distributing private brand merchandise on a European scale "under the label Spar Europ. The Spar groups which are now active in fourteen European countries are aiming at developing a range of products of consistent quality at competitive prices with a label which will be recognized by customers in any European country."[9] This is consistent with American experience, and American marketers in Europe should be among the leaders in developing European brands as the opportunities grow for mass marketing on a continental scale.

Slow Change

Actually, there is relatively little European brand standardization in consumer nondurables, as compared with the American market. Continuing language and market differences hinder the development of Europe-wide brands. Inertia plays some role also, though standardization efforts are under way in many firms.

As noted earlier, most consumer goods firms and a few industrial marketers had some diversity of brand names in Europe. There were varied causes for this: new brands acquired through joint ventures or acquisition, deliberate policy or accidential historical development, bad connotation or lack of pronounceability of the American brand name, loss through prior registration by another. None was happy about the array of brands (though the degree of dissatisfaction varied), and most were making some efforts at standardization. Those who used American brand names had no problem. This included a majority of the industrial marketers and a few consumer goods firms.

Efforts Toward Brand Standardization

The efforts toward brand standardization depend in part on the cause of diversity. Where the name has a bad connotation in some countries, a new brand can be found for just those countries or else one that can be common for all countries. The latter course would, however, mean the loss of good will for the original name. Use of more than one brand would seem to be advisable here. With prior registration by another, the alternatives and solution are the same, though there is the possibility of buying back the company's rights to the name. This involves a balancing of costs and gains. The pronunciation problem and solution are again similar but probably more amenable to adjustment. One respondent firm changed just one letter in a nine-letter brand name to facilitate its pronunciation by German consumers.

Where diversity is the result of deliberate policy, presumably the company figures the gains in national markets to be more important than standardization internationally. When this is true, there can still be many common features linking the product. The design, color, and size of the

package and label can be the same, including the company
name and symbol as family brand--in fact, everything can
be the same except the brand name and the language on the
package or label. Thus, one executive whose firm had a
variety of brands in different Member Countries said, "Brand
name is less important than design, and we're attaining consistency of design. Ours are supermarket products and the
visual image is most important--on the shelf or in advertising." He said the Common Market had accentuated his firm's
drive for standardization.

Where diversity of brands is the result of historical development or accident, the results are likely to be less than
optimal and gains from standardization more likely. Some
European subsidiaries began operations as national concerns
with no thought of international markets. The branding situation that developed is usually not suited to the facts of
economic integration. This is similar to the earlier situation in the American market where improvements in transportation and communication have extended the geographical
coverage of former regional brands. In the Common Market, increased consumer mobility and improved communication are reinforced by economic integration. Therefore,
in the EEC, as in the United States, "it can reasonably be
assumed these days that any brand may be sold throughout
the national market eventually."[10]

Because of such historical factors in pre-Common Market days, one company had one of its brands representing
three different products in three different countries. It now
has its international staff working on the development of international brands. A name such as "Royal" might need to
be "La Roy" in another country, the respondent suggested.
The transition would have to be carefully planned to minimize
the loss of good will attached to the brand being changed.

Where diversity comes through acquisition or joint venture, there is probably too much good will attached to the
European brand and too little to the new American brand
to make any sudden changes feasible. One food marketer
noted: "Our name and symbol aren't important. What
counts is getting in the market with a product. You keep
the name you acquired as that is part of what you paid for."
This firm planned acquisitions in two more Member Coun-

tries   and then expected to begin a program of standardization
and rationalization. However, since the acquired brands are
most frequently national in scope and the American marketer
usually plans EEC or Europe-wide operations, planning for
standardization must begin. The problems and calculations
in standardization of brands in Europe are, of course, similar
to those faced by marketers in America when they consolidate
brands.[11]

While standardization of brands is increasing in Europe,
and American marketers will want to be among the leaders
in this, there shouldn't be a rigid program. The firm, in
considering its particular situation, should analyze the possibilities and carefully weigh the long-run gains and losses.

The best program for a firm might well stop short of
complete standardization. As one respondent wisely noted:
"We don't want a weak brand name just because it's regis-
trable everywhere." And whatever diversity may continue,
there are possibilities for unifying the company image in
other ways: Packaging and labeling can be alike in design,
colors, sizes; the company symbol can tie the different
company products together; the company name can serve as
a family brand link. Several companies were using one or
more of these approaches. As another example, the United
States Rubber Company, after a two-year study, adopted a
new worldwide trade name as its marketing umbrella for
products from diverse country sources. A design incorporating the name UNIROYAL is used with the name of the subsidiary underneath.[12] For a new product, the task should
be easier as there can be consideration given to European
(or global) requirements before choosing a name. There
will be more emphasis on the international suitability of brand
names as contrasted to particular national fitness.

PACKAGING AND LABELING

The promotional aspects of packaging and labeling should
undergo adjustments similar to those in the rest of the promotional program, as discussed above under "Advertising" and
"Branding." Nevertheless, because there are distinctive elements in each part of the promotional program, it is useful
to consider them separately.

Adaptation of Packages and Labels

Just as desire for greater market penetration leads to adapting the product and promotion to European market requirements, so packaging and labeling should be Europeanized, since they are promotional tools as well as part of the product ("bundle of utilities") received by the customer. Package adaptation is generally necessary because the European market is not a duplicate of the American. Languages differ, and there are several of them. Where the copy on the package or label has a message to communicate, a language change is needed. A 1966 survey of French housewives showed that most disliked foreign labels on imported goods.[13]

Because of lower incomes and smaller storage facilities, the European consumer is apt to want a smaller package. The European retail outlet is usually small, and the retailer has less money and space for inventory. This reinforces the need for smaller packages at lower prices and may also mean smaller cases with fewer packages. The growth of self-service in Europe, following the American experience, emphasizes the importance of the package as salesman--a salesman speaking to the European consumer. National regulations may require package adaptation; or it may be forced by competitive practice, especially when the American firm is a newcomer in the European market. As with other adjustments, adaptation of package and label is facilitated with local manufacture.

Experience in Adaptation

The packaging problem is most important to manufacturers of consumer nondurables, but it does affect other marketers also. Of the respondent firms using packaging in some form, all but one had modified it for Europe--if only as to language. The one exception operated through export and felt the American image (including "Made in U. S. A. ") was very important in its line. For Europe, this firm omitted only the dollar price, which was printed on the package in America. For many firms, package adaptation came with local manufacture when a greater market penetration was desired than had been obtained with exports.

Most American manufacturers like to have their European packages resemble the American as much as possible. This assists international standardization and integration of promotion. A few companies were able to use the American package with only a language change. The products included photographic film, chewing gum, cosmetics, canned soups, and parts for farm equipment. For one prepared food product, however, the producer was considering adoption of a smaller package as being more appropriate for the Common Market. (The company was not being as successful as it had expected with its regular American package.)

One of the most common adaptations was a reduction in package size. A majority of the manufacturers of nondurables had done this on the Continent. Getting a lower shelf price is usually the motivation for a smaller package. A paper products firm reduced an individual item to two thirds of its American size and then put seventy-five items in the package instead of 100 or 200 as in the United States. On another product, it put ten to a package instead of twelve or twenty-four. A package of crackers is six to seven ounces rather than a pound. Even case sizes are apt to be smaller because of distribution requirements. A food company had cases of twelve cans in some Member Countries and twenty-four cans in others, whereas its standard American case is forty-eight cans.

While the need for a lower shelf price and national regulations are major causes of adaptation, there can be other factors in particular cases. The situation of a drug manufacturer illustrates some of these. The company said there were four variables affecting its package sizes: (1) government reimbursement practices, (2) doctors' preferences, (3) patients' needs, (4) competitive practices. These led to different sizes in different countries.

National regulations can affect labels as well as packages, especially on food, drug, and cosmetic products. These regulations vary from country to country. For example, imported goods that fail to conform to the German marking and labeling regulations are refused entry into the Federal Republic of Germany. Toilet soap sold in Belgium must show on the wrapper the fatty acid content by weight followed by the letters A. G. --Acide Gras. This type of adaptation is involuntary but no less necessary than the more strategic adjustments mentioned above. A pharmaceutical firm had a European medical doctor in charge of translating and adapting copy for labels and inserts.

Occasionally, adaptation is more accidental than strategic. Various subsidiaries may have followed their own paths, and the same might be true of licensees or joint-venture partners. However, the American firm should be alert to maximum use of packaging as a sales tool. This would give it a competitive advantage as the Europeans have been slower to see the promotional aspects of packaging.[14] At the same time, Europeans are sophisticated about new packaging ideas; and the American company may well incorporate these ideas as well as local market requirements into its European package. Two firms had even found new packaging ideas for America from their European operations. As with all adaptation, local market research is an initial step and local market testing a final step.

Standardization of Packages and Labels

While adaptation of package is necessary and desirable for most American marketers in Europe, it is also desirable to have the greatest uniformity possible within Europe. The great growth in intra-EEC trade means increased sales across national borders by the individual firm. With many American firms operating in more than one Member Country, it is desirable that the products from different sources look alike. The extensive international travel of Europeans is a second reason for seeking standardization of package, just as consumer mobility in America forces a standard package for the national market. Both goods and consumers travel more in Europe today.

Improved communications and company programs for standardization of products, brands, and advertising are a third force for package uniformity. Although national regulations on packaging vary, the Rome Treaty plan to harmonize these differences should make standardization more feasible. Efforts of trade associations reinforce the official community activity toward eliminating differences. Of course, the gains and costs of standardization (both in production and marketing) should be weighed against those of variety.

Labeling

One aid to standardization of labels would seem to be multilingual copy. Some of the diverse national requirements could
be met while permitting the use of a single package for the
whole market. However, the experience of the respondent
firms doesn't seem to favor this yet. Apart from the multilingual Belgian and Swiss markets, packages were printed
primarily in one language. A packaging firm selling to European industry said this held for European companies also.
Of course, some firms had not given much thought to a multilingual approach.

A chemical firm used multilingual labeling and found no
problem in the industrial market. Weight was in pounds and
kilograms. A multilingual package was used for inner tubes.
locks, and some other items where very little copy was
needed on the package. It was little used in consumer nondurables, where packaging is most important. One veteran
European marketer had tried some multilingual packages,
but found the effort abortive with a negative effect. "Except
in Belgium and Switzerland, which are multilingual anyway,
it clutters up the package and makes it look like a foreign
product. We don't want to lose that local identity. It pays."
Another felt the major drawback of national packages was
just the package-inventory problem.

Related to this attempt at standardization is another in
which one language is used on the package in all countries.
In some cases, English copy may not be detrimental but even
beneficial. Where little copy is needed and an American (or
English) image is desired, this may be an attractive method.
Some European firms use English for this reason. There
is a European package of chewing gum with an American name
and all English copy except for "Tirez" (pull). An American cosmetics firm wants to put out one of its products with
French copy only to get a French image. These examples
are in the minority but should gradually increase.

For certain products, multilingual inserts give further
information or directions to supplement the limited copy on
the package. Examples of this are photographic film, ethical
and proprietary medicines, and a four-language service man-
ual for refrigerator exports. Somewhat differently, an Ital-

ian manufacturer sold a prepared food product with minimal copy in one language and an illustration of the product plus a pattern including the flags of all the European countries in which the product was sold. This presumably helped to create a European image.

The conclusion on labeling for the EEC is that national labels remain the general rule in consumer goods. However, opportunities are improving for greater standardization.

Packaging

In addition to these attempts at uniformity of labeling, packaging standardization efforts are being made by American manufacturers in Europe. While taking cognizance of legislative and language requirements, much can still be done to make packages more uniform. Again, the first step is to study the situation and look for the common denominators-- not the differences. Many national peculiarities must eventually fade before the demands of a mass European market. (Even two American drug manufacturers were optimistic about harmonizing of laws in their highly regulated industry.) According to a French packaging authority, European packaging is paralleling advances in the U.S. He notes the changing pattern of retail distribution (increasing number of self-service stores and supermarkets) and the rising standard of European living. [15] These developments are common to most of the EEC and constitute a pressure for more standardized packages.

Many of the differences in the packages of American manufacturers in Europe arose because of operations conducted in the context of separate national markets with little international selling. Since many of these differences have no intrinsic necessity, they can and should now be eliminated in the context of the Common Market. There is now a need for standardization, whereas it was unimportant before in national markets. Implementation may need to be gradual, but it should be started where possible. Even though standardization may not be complete, much progress can often be made.

A few examples of respondent firms illustrate some of the approaches to standardization in packaging. One company,

which is centralizing its Common Market production in the
Netherlands, has begun a program to eliminate the difference
in the size, shape, color, cap, and design of its packages--
even though product formulas and brands often vary nationally. Other firms have similar goals, but one noted: "We
are working slowly and avoiding revolutionary changes. We
made serious errors once when we got carried away with a
passion for uniformity for its own sake." Once an international package has been decided on in this firm, each country
subsidiary can decide the timing for adoption--but it must
adopt.

A food marketer had no less than three different sizes of
packages for one of its leading items--about one ounce difference between them. One was from its English plant,
another from its French plant, and the other from its Italian licensee. All three packages were developed at different times in different markets, but are now often in over-
lapping market areas. Nonrenewal of the licensing contract
will eliminate one, and the other two will be standardized.

WARRANTIES AND SERVICE POLICIES

Warranties and service policies have both protective and
promotional aspects, but only the latter will be discussed here.
The increased competition in the integrated market might be
expected to lead to more liberal warranties and service policies. Excess capacity in many lines and a buyers' market
mean a greater need for such promotional tools. The fact
that American companies are newer in the market and are
aiming for an expanding share of European business also suggests liberalized warranty and service policies. To the extent that American manufacturers' products have a technical
edge, the use of more liberal warranties would be justified
and would not mean that they're proceeding from weakness.
The expanded warranties on the 1967-model cars in the
United States are a relevant example.

The growth of intra-EEC trade and travel implies here
the need for growing standardization. Warranties and service policies should become more uniform throughout the
Common Market as they are in the geographically larger
American market. If these policies were to be promoted in
an EEC-wide promotion, such uniformity would be neces-

sary as it is in the United States. One vice-president with
several decades of international experience said he had one
firm conviction: "If a company in industrial goods studies
the situation well, it is possible to have the same products,
selling methods, etc., all over the world."

Warranties

Liberalization

Warranties apply particularly to mechanical products but
have some application to others, such as drugs or floor tile.
For many products there is just an implied warranty of satisfaction or that the product meets the specifications stated.
Increased competition and other reasons given above suggest
liberalized warranties by American manufacturers in the
EEC. This suggestion assumes that warranties will be used
competitively. There is some difference in American practice in the EEC on this matter. Half of the firms using warranties had the same one in Europe as in America. While
the warranties were competitive, there were no changes resulting from new conditions in Europe. Often there was a
technological edge of the American company; and this edge
plus being competitive on warranty and other matters, gave
the company a satisfactory market position. Products covered
here included materials-handling equipment, business machines,
electrical equipment, floor tiles, and appliances.

One company found that its standard American warranty
(on exports) was generally more liberal than European warranties, and it was promoted by the local distributor. "On
consumer durables, American products have the edge. We're
the Cadillacs of the field and the consumer will often pay a
premium. There has been no Common Market impact as we
led in warranties before. The Europeans must come up to
ours, though they're not happy about giving guarantees."

Another group of firms did respond to competition in warranties. Products here included automobiles, tires, and farm
equipment; and in each case the competition was the major variable affecting warranties. The firms usually did what was
necessary to meet competition. One said, "We're not a leader but a follower in warranties. However, we do promote
them more than our competitors." Another had two alternative

strategies, depending on the situation in a particular country:
"If we can be first, we tell the story and get the benefit of
leadership. Elsewhere, we try not to disturb the market."
Dominant national producers are often a restraining force.

Uniformity

As to the increased uniformity of warranties expected in
the EEC, there was no evidence of change. Firms using
their American warranty in Europe had been using a standard
approach since before the EEC began. Firms adapting to
local competitive conditions continued to vary warranties on
a national basis. In the EEC, in automobiles, farm equipment, and tires, the major national markets are dominated
by national producers; and there is no common situation
throughout the market. Trade associations are making ef-
fors toward standardization, often for a greater-than-EEC
area. In one case, however, the leading French producer
was blocking such efforts in the EEC, feeling they would
benefit the Americans more than the Europeans. Though the
logic of a common market implies standardization, the realities of the Common Market do not warrant it for all.

Service Policies

Liberalization

Service policies here refer only to post-sale service.
Pre-sale service will be discussed below under "Personal Selling," In America, applicance manufacturers and industrial
marketers have had to expand and improve their after-sale
service, both because of competitive pressure and the need
to maintain customer good will. The desire for a larger market share in Europe has led many American manufacturers
to a similar expansion of their European service activities.

Many manufacturers have established or expanded service or sales-service staffs in Europe. Their primary goal
was to expand sales through pre-sales service such as application service or systems development, but there was almost always an accompanying increase in after-sale service
as well. As a chemical company respondent noted, "We
really offer continuous service. First, to show him how to
use the product, and then to assure his continued profitable

use so that we keep him as a customer. We're operating in
Europe now just as we operate here." A farm equipment manufacturer noted that, "Our customers get very good service as
all our European sales are on long-run financing. If the customer is dissatisfied, he can leave the equipment at the distributor's door."

Service is heavily promoted by American manufacturers
in Europe. They feel that it is an important competitive tool
that   gives them an edge in the market. An electrical equipment firm was establishing a new-product division in Europe
and began by opening and promoting local service facilities.
An applicance firm had done marketing research before greatly
expanding its applicance line in its own retail outlets. There
was a very favorable consumer response in the survey. The
reason: "Good service."

Standardization

There is somewhat greater standardization in service
policies than with warranties. After-sale service is more
closely related to maintaining the consumers' good will than
is the warranty. The two are related, but action speaks
louder than words; and the warranty is words, while the service is action. An automobile marketer noted, "Our service
programs are basically the same. Competition is not a factor here as in warranty." As part of its standardization
program, this firm is adopting a uniform service identification in Europe so that travelers can find service easily.

Several firms had schools or training centers for service-
men, dealers, or licensees. This was especially true for
equipment manufacturers, but a marketer of flooring and ceiling materials also had training schools in Germany, Paris,
and one on the road. Such training helps to assure uniform,
competent service and to maintain customer good will. An
equipment manufacturer had sales-service men from its Swiss
agency checking up on distributors and customers to achieve
the same goals.

With licensees, the service requirements are spelled out
in the contract; but unless there is some control, there is
no assurance that the same level of service is offered by different licensees. Such control has usually increased with en-

larged European service staffs of American licensors. With
some very technical equipment, such as computers or elevators,
uniform service contracts are sold with the equipment and
standard qualified service is available from the manufacturer.

There are still some examples of diversity of service in
the EEC operations of American firms. Many have separate
national subsidiaries; and even though policies are the same,
administration may differ. In other cases, there is no uniform policy. A tire marketer said its adjustment policies
varied not only nationally but even within countries. Competition is a major factor causing such variation, but differing
conditions of product use may also be important. The latter
reason was noted especially by a farm equipment manufacturer.
It varied the number of months of free service according to
local-use conditions and local competition. It made regular
comparisons of service costs between regions to assure that
the variations were not too great.

PERSONAL SELLING

Personal selling is especially important in the industrial
market, where it usually bears the brunt of the promotional
burden. It is, however, a form of promotion used in some
degree by all American marketers in Europe. The changes
occurring in the Common Market should lead to changes in the
role and nature of personal selling in American manufacturers'
marketing programs. Increased competition and a buyers'
market mean that a harder, more skillful selling job is needed
to maintain market share. The increased ambitions of American marketers in Europe, plus the initiation or expansion of
local manufacturing, require new and greater salesmanship.
As the Common Market becomes a unified market, there
should be an adjustment of sales territories according to
natural sales areas rather than strictly political boundaries.
Along with this territorial adjustment could be an increasing
use of multilingual salesmen for the multinational market.

Consumer Goods

Although advertising plays a relatively greater role in
selling to consumers, personal salesmanship is important
in reaching wholesalers and retailers. With the restrictions

on advertising, the lack of wide media coverage and commercial television, and the proportionately greater number of retailers in Europe, the salesman's role is magnified.

Adaptation and Expansion

American consumer marketers in Europe have generally adapted their personal selling promotion to the new competitive and market conditions. Their American experience was usually helpful, and one noted that conditions are like those in America twenty years ago. Most try to use their United States approach as far as possible, and this is true for products ranging from soft drinks and chewing gum to consumer durables.

The major adaptation is from "mere" selling or order taking to more aggressive merchandising and missionary selling. One respondent said, "Our salesmen's training now is more marketing oriented toward knowing and meeting distributor needs, rather than just loading the retailer." In the fight for shelf space and display, the salesman must be able to show the retailer how he benefits from cooperating with the manufacturer. This involves some knowledge of margins and turnover of various products and how the manufacturer's advertising pre-sells the product. One respondent following this approach said that change was slow because of the difficulty of covering such a great number of retailers and doing a good job with all of them.

Along with a stronger marketing orientation in personal selling, there has been an increase in sales support activity (in addition to advertising). "Trade relations" or "public relations" by executives or special personnel was undertaken by some manufacturers. There was an increase in the preparation of materials for the salesmen and for point-of-purchase display. A tire manufacturer expanded its fleet-analysis service, and an automobile marketer began a training program for its dealers, covering such new European problems as trade-ins and a buyers' market. Others paid closer attention to training of salesmen.

Many expressed dissatisfaction with the quality of wholesaling available in Europe. Wholesaling is generally less developed in Europe, partly because the European manufacturer doesn't like to use wholesalers. It would seem, however, that there should be improvement here as the wholesaler can be a valuable help to the manufacturer in reaching out to the expanded markets available with economic integration. Difficulty in getting qualified sales personnel should reinforce the value of the wholesaler. One firm, after an on-the-spot study, did switch from direct distribution to the use of wholesalers. It felt that this was the most efficient way to get the wider coverage needed.

Two firms in the paper products field illustrate some of the adjustments made in the use of personal selling. One company continued using the sales organizations of its joint-venture partners. These partners continued their work of sales management with the American firm acting, in effect, as marketing consultant. It followed its American pattern of selective distribution, which it claimed permitted a smaller sales force and more intensive cultivation.

The other firm had been using direct distribution in France. This had been encouraged by the form of commission payment that allowed 5 per cent commission on sales to retailers versus 2 per cent on sales to wholesalers. After a study by the resident American manager, this firm switched salesmen's renumeration to a salary basis for better control over their activities and began distributing through wholesalers. It felt 100 per cent distribution was necessary for volume and that this was impossible with its own sales force.

No Change

Some firms made little change in their use of personal selling. This was especially true for firms newer in the market or with a lesser commitment, such as export, licensing, or joint venture. Where part of the market was serviced by exports, there was often a continuation of the old distributor arrangement. This was more or less satisfactory, depending on competitive conditions. One food marketer importing into Germany complained of the difficulty of competing against Unilever with its large fleet of truck driver-salesmen. Another food company, which considers its large American sales force as a major competitive weapon, is continuing with the small sales forces of the acquired European firms. Changes are expected as the firm gains personnel and experience and takes stronger control of European operations.

As to a redefining of sales territories or an increasing use of multilingual salesmen in view of the Common Market, there is little evidence. The firms are still distributing and selling on a national basis with national salesmen. Most are skeptical about any change in this in the foreseeable future. Chapter 5, "Distribution Adjustments," discusses this further.

Industrial Goods

Since personal selling is more important here than with consumer goods, it is not surprising that there have been greater adjustments in personal sales promotion by industrial than by consumer marketers. The major trends observed are toward greater control of selling and distribution and toward a customer or marketing orientation in selling.

The increased interest and ambition of American industrial marketers in Europe have been accompanied by a desire for greater control of European operations, including the crucial selling task. In the case of switching from exports to local manufacture, it frequently means the replacement of the importer-distributor by the company's own sales organization. A chemical company considers that its advantage is often in its sales-service activities, rather than in the basic product itself. When it established European manufacturing, it found one of its hardest problems was to get enough qualified Europeans for the extensive sales-service activity it felt was necessary. It now has 120 Americans in Europe in sales and administration, and training is one of their main responsibilities (total staff is 5,000). The European director noted: "Selling and marketing are the big jobs. Manufacturing is the same all over."

Other firms who had been operating through European manufacture well before the Common Market began were also moving toward greater control. A packaging manufacturer dropped commission agents to sell through its own trained sales force. The Americans it has in Europe all have a background in sales and marketing and are applying their sales approach to the EEC market. Several companies were dissatisfied with the caliber of personal selling done by distributors and agents. Thus, a farm equipment manufacturer started a training program and was trying to get control of distribution. It was dropping agents but did not yet have its own sales force. An electrical equipment company was using its own product specialists in part to aid and inspire distributors' salesmanship.

Besides increasing control of selling, the other adjustment noted among a majority of the industrial marketers is an upgrading of the selling task. New competition, a buyers' market, and more aggressive goals led to a sharpening of this important tool of personal selling. This upgrading took a variety of forms but always included an increase in customer orientation, i.e., not just selling a product to the customer, but rather determining his needs and how the company's products could meet those needs.

A few examples will show some of the variety of upgrading and intensification of personal selling. A packaging manufacturer was stressing the tailoring of its products to the particular needs of each customer and was calling its new, trained salesmen "packaging engineers." One firm loaned technical representatives to subsidiaries for new-product introduction. The idea took, and the subsidiaries hired their own "tech reps." A chemical company said: "We now have higher-level salesmen. They're no longer generalists selling 700 products but specialists by product or industry. They must know both product and industry and how they fit together." This firm also put supporting specialists (i.e., chemists, engineers) in Europe.

This upgrading extends even to operations by export or licensing. An electrical equipment exporter had four regional salesmen for the Continent. With the advent of the Common Market, he retained the regional men but added a sizable staff of product specialists in Switzerland. They specialize by products (exports) for all of Europe, work with distributors, and occassionally go with the salesmen of licensees. While there is little control over licensee selling, the licensee's salesmen may be trained and receive assistance from the licensor. As one executive noted: "We've got to send the same kind of men to our foreign customers that we send to Bethlehem Steel. They won't settle for less. We often have to reach into various domestic divisions to find the experts we need."

With industrial marketers there is more international selling (i.e., salesmen covering more than one national market) than is true for consumer goods marketers. However, even here much selling is to national markets by national sales-men; and several respondents felt that a change would not be feasible for a long time. While products and technology are more and more international, the selling task seems to re-main quite personal and, therefore, affected by national influ-ences. To the extent that there is international selling, it usually requires multilingual salesmen. One company had been selling internationally long before the Common Market and found that getting bilingual salesmen was no problem in Europe.

CONCLUSIONS

The general expectations on American manufacturers' promotional activities in the EEC were: first, an increased use of promotional tools in the more competitive market; second, a more standardized or uniform approach in the Com-mon Market. The actual developments are summarized be-low.

Advertising

There has occurred the expected increase in American advertising outlays in the EEC, in many cases relative to sales as well as absolutely. The major reasons are in-creased competition and higher market goals by American companies.

Uniformity of advertising is scarcely to be found as there are continuing and important differences between national markets. Nonetheless, many firms are taking steps toward standardization of advertising and are finding that many form-er disparities can be eliminated without danger to advertising effectiveness. A careful but conscientious effort will pay off as market-wide media develop.

Branding

The increased American business interest in Europe, re-sulting in large part from the Common Market, should lead to an adaptation of American brand names in Europe. This has not been notable in the industrial market, where brand is re-

latively unimportant. However, in consumer goods brands
tend to be quite "Europeanized." In part, this antedates the
Rome Treaty; but increased American operations since 1957
have meant many new Europeanized products and brands.

Standardization of brands has been occurring rather slowly
for somewhat the same reasons as in advertising. There is
a further problem here concerning the good will adhering to
different national brands. However, companies are progressing toward wider brand coverage.

Packaging and Labeling

Packages and labels have been extensively adapted to
Europe, partly because of market requirements and partly
because of legal requirements. Smaller size is the most
frequent package difference.

Adaptation of packages and labels within different national
requirements usually mean a lack of uniformity. However,
American firms have made progress in standardizing both
the appearance and nature of their European labels and packages.

Warranties and Service Policies

There has been no notable liberalization of warranties by
American companies in Europe. They have felt competitive
generally with existing practice. However, industrial goods
firms have stepped up their post-sale service as a competitive weapon.

Warranties have not become more uniform in the EEC
in spite of occasional efforts in that direction. Service
policies, on the other hand, are quite standard. The reason for this is the need to maintain the same degree of customer satisfaction in each Member Country, regardless of
competition.

Personal Selling

Personal selling has increased in importance both in consumer goods and industrial goods (missionary selling in consumer goods). There has also been an upgrading of the selling

task and an increase in sales-support activity in the more competitive market.

Although sales across national boundaries are up greatly in the Common Market, personal selling is still done largely by nationals in their national market. The use of multilingual international salesmen has not increased much and is not likely to in the near future.

NOTES TO CHAPTER 4

1. "Advertising Outpaces the European Economy, " The International Advertiser, II, 5 (May, 1961), 12.

2. "Hard-Driving Americans Push Small Firms to the Wall, " German International, VI, 4 (April 30, 1962), 20.

3. International Commerce, LXX, 5 (February 3, 1964), inside front cover.

4. Erik Elinder, "How International Can Advertising Be? " International Handbook of Advertising, ed. S. Watson Dunn (New York: McGraw-Hill Book Co. , Inc. , 1964), pp. 59-71

5. "World May Be Small; It's Still a Marketing Problem, " Advertising Age, XXXV, 8 (February 24, 1964), 174.

6. "World Business, " Time, June 1, 1962, p. 78.

7. Maynard D. Phelps and J. Howard Westing, Marketing Management (rev. ed. ; Homewood, Ill. : Richard D. Irwin, Inc. , 1960), p. 88.

8. "Unilever on Europe, " International Management, XVIII, 6 (June, 1963), 2.

9. Retail News Letter, International Association of Department Stores, Paris, No. 83 (May, 1964), p. 2.

10. Phelps and Westing, op. cit., p. 110.

11. Ibid., pp. 110-11.

12. "One Name to Girdle the Globe," Business Week, August 1, 1964, p. 74.

13. "French Housewives View Food Packages," Printers' Ink, February 11, 1966, p. 56.

14. Braxton Pollard, "International Advertising in the 60's," Export Trade, LXXXIV, 26 (January 29, 1962), 11.

15. "Europeans Adopting Packages a la U.S.," Printers' Ink, June 19, 1966, pp. 32-33.

CHAPTER **5** DISTRIBUTION
ADJUSTMENTS

The many economic changes occurring in Western Europe
call for multiple adjustments by the American manufacturer
marketing in Europe. Changes in product policy and promotion have been discussed. Further adaptation is to be expected in distribution practice. The distribution channels (or
links between the manufacturer and the customer) that were
used in a sellers' market in various national markets may
not be appropriate in the new buyers' market of the integrated
economies. American manufacturers' increasing emphasis
on local production in place of exports may call for accompanying changes in distribution. The desire of American
manufacturers for a greater share of European business can
also call for distribution changes suitable for this new goal,
and increased competition may force such changes. The evolution of wholesaling and retailing in Europe may make changes
feasible and desirable.[1]

The distribution practices of American manufacturers
in the EEC were investigated primarily to determine whether
three types of adjustment had taken place: first, whether
economic integration has led to more international patterns
of distribution; second, whether increased European competition has led to greater cooperation with distributive intermediaries or to greater control over distribution; third,
whether economic integration and the common transport policy of the EEC have led to changes in physical distribution.

INTERNATIONAL DISTRIBUTION

When and if the six Member Countries of the EEC reach
a true common market, distribution patterns should be orga-
nized on a rational basis to serve natural market areas, as
in the United States, rather than being shaped by national political boundaries. Because distribution according to natural
market areas is more efficient and because that is what they
are accustomed to in America, one would expect American

manufacturers to be implementing such economically rational
distribution as conditions permit.

Two definitions may be in order here. What is meant
in this discussion by "national distribution" is the organization of a manufacturer's distribution channels or intermediaries on a national basis. That is, the manufacturer has a
particular distribution setup in France, a separate--though
perhaps similar--one in Germany, etc. Distribution channels can thus be national even though production is centralized
for the whole Common Market.

"International distribution" then would be organization of
distribution channels on a market-wide basis, or according
to natural market areas--disregarding national political boundaries. A particular distribution channel would include two
or more Member Countries.

Several conditions favor the establishment of rational distribution on a Common Market-wide basis. If a company's
products are identical throughout the EEC, if its advertising,
branding, and packaging are standardized, and if there is
centralization of its production for the EEC, distribution
should follow natural market areas. As the heart supplies
each part of the body according to its needs, so should the
distribution of products occur freely in a common market.
Tariffs and other restrictions are like tourniquets hindering
the normal flow. As these restrictions are removed with
integration, the natural flow should eventually take place.

On the other hand, other conditions may impede the development of more rational international distribution. If
a company's products and promotion differ nationally, if
production is on a national basis, if there are established
national distribution subsidiaries with a vested interest in
remaining national, and if there are continuing national market differences, distribution may remain largely national.
Cost considerations may enter the picture, too, since the
anticipated gains from any change should be weighed against
its cost.

National Distribution Continues

Chapter 2 dealt with the rationalization of production that has occurred in the Common Market. Many American manufacturers have established one production source for the whole EEC. Others, with plants in several Member Countries, have specialized production at these plants so that each one produces one part of the product line for the whole EEC rather than the complete line for a national market. In contrast, there has been no similar rationalization of distribution on a Common Market-wide basis. American manufacturers are using national distribution channels almost exclusively.

This continued emphasis on national distribution channels is illustrated by American companies in all product lines. For example, a manufacturer of home-care products is centralizing Common Market production in the Netherlands, but is retaining strictly national distribution. There are several reasons for this. The conditions of product use vary somewhat from country to country, and the product is found in different types of outlets in different countries. The continuation of distinctive national characteristics is another factor. The respondent, who had spent several years in Europe, noted: "There is no possibility of Common Market-wide distribution in this century. A Frenchman is a Frenchman with an intellectual, cultural, and linguistic heritage of over one thousand years. The Rome Treaty is a politico-economic document and won't soon change national psychologies."

An automobile firm also has one production source in the EEC. The Common Market allows greater international sales from this plant and permitted the firm to open a large assembly plant in another Member Country. However, all the distribution organizations are national. Though the subject is under study, no changes are foreseen soon. Differing national taxes and regulations on automobiles are important reasons for maintaing national distribution. The remaining internal tariffs cause a further problem. There is the tariff expense plus the intermediate step of sending the car to a tariff depot, which results in additional cost. The complete removal of internal tariffs and harmonizing of regulations, when they occur, will facilitate a more international distribution pattern.

A manufacturer of business machines has standardized products throughout Europe, and each of its European plants produces one product for the whole market. Distribution, however, is national. When a system or group of related machines is sold, elements from other countries are assembled at the plant in the country of sale. European headquarters coordinates the operation, but the sales work and distribution are done within the country by nationals. The reason for national distribution here was not differences in product or use habits or national regulations as in the previous examples. The crucial factor was the differences in national character and personality. A vice-president said: "National differences will continue to be major, especially in people-to-people dealings. The day that a German will work in France and vice versa is far off. You can't use salesmen in other countries. Only unskilled labor will really travel." Manufacturers of such diverse products as sewing machines and chewing gum also mentioned the importance of differences in national character as affecting distribution channels.

Steps Toward International Distribution

Though American use of multinational distribution channels is rare, preliminary steps in that direction are being undertaken. The continued progress of European integration and growth of a European market with products, promotion, and consumers flowing over national boundaries must eventually lead to less national but more rational distribution patterns according to natural market areas. Many European retail and wholesale chains and department stores are beginning to purchase irrespective of national source. Another internationalizing influence is the generation of youth, who are more "Europe-minded" than their elders. Therefore, it is not surprising that many American manufacturers are studying their distribution channels to find patterns appropriate to the changing requirements. More efficient distribution will benefit both manufacturers and consumers.

Not only is distribution being studied, but measures to implement a more international system of distribution are in evidence. Several companies have European sales subsidiaries or departments at European headquarters, which coordinate sales in Europe. These may cover just nonplant countries, the whole EEC, or all of Europe and more, but

they are notable in that they represent a first effort at international coordination of distribution and source allocation.
While the distribution pattern of these companies is still
national, there is at least multinational consideration of the
problems involved; and this experience should aid in establishing a more international distribution pattern when conditions warrant.

As an example, a chemical company has a Swiss subsidiary in charge of all its European sales. The subsidiary sells
to national distributors but "quarterbacks" the company's
sales for all of Europe--from both European and American
plants. It acts as central staff for Europe on advertising,
billing, and sales. The European director said: "Perhaps we
will have real international distribution in twenty years. The
national companies would then be regional sales offices like
Chicago or San Francisco in the United States." This solution would have the advantage of avoiding the elimination of
national organizations in which vested interests have arisen.
Another chemical company has a long-range plan for its European headquarters to be its selling agent for all of Europe.
However, it sells through national agents at present and has
just established another national subsidiary to market nylon
in Germany.

There are other evidences of internationalization of distribution as American manufacturers seek to compete more
effectively and profitably in Europe. The marketing research
director of a rubber company studied its European distribution pattern. Though its distribution is still primarily national, the company changed its sales districts and reduced the
number of warehouses in line with a more strategic approach
to natural market areas. A food manufacturer dropped several national agents when it signed a licensing agreement with
an Italian firm with a multinational distribution network. After
the Rome Treaty, the company began a program of acquisitions in the EEC and expects to rationalize both its production and distribution when it has consolidated and digested its
acquisitions. Another food firm with many European plants
said that when all the barriers were gone it would probably
have specialization of production by plant with distribution
centers for the whole EEC.

Operating through licensees can hinder rationalization of distribution. For example, an equipment manufacturer was selling a lot more internationally since integration began but faced a special problem. Its French licensee was competing against its other European plants outside of France. The company was able to coordinate sales and distribution of its own production, but couldn't control those of the licensee.

INCREASED CONTROL AND COOPERATION IN DISTRIBUTION

Control

The increased American interest in European business has meant a desire for greater control of European operations, including distribution. The sellers' market in Europe in the first postwar decade did not require much selling effort by American manufacturers. European sales were often a small per cent of total volume anyway. A profit squeeze in the United States in the late 1950's combined with European recovery and integration and a buyers' market led to greater diligence in the conduct of European business. This new effort pertained not only to manufacturers' own organizations but also to those who worked with them in reaching the consumer--the distributors or middlemen.

Unfortunately for the manufacturer, distributors are usually independent middlemen. Often the only way a manufacturer can increase his control is by doing more of the distribution himself, that is, by using a more direct channel. American manufacturers are frequently able to use a more direct channel in America than in Europe because of their relatively greater volume here. This indirect channel in Europe may put them at a serious competitive disadvantage with larger European firms. The major distribution problem is often inability to go direct with current volume. One respondent mentioned the difficulty of competing against Unilever with its large fleet of truck driver-salesmen covering all the retailers. He noted that Germany has 300,000 grocery stores; but chains are relatively unimportant there, so the number of sales contacts is very great. A new manufacturer can have difficulty breaking in against established competition.

Most American manufacturers in Europe wish to exert greater control over the distribution of their products, and many have succeeded--but only by doing more of the distribution themselves. When they have established local manufacturing in a Member Country, many manufacturers have been able to replace independent distributors there. The local plant usually becomes the distributor for that country. The growth of chains that like to buy directly has been a help to some companies. A clothing firm finds that its large Dutch customers like to deal directly with the manufacturer.

Manufacturers of consumers durables are especially interested in control of distribution because the distributor-customer relationship is more important here than with items sold in supermarkets. One of Chrysler's major tasks in Europe was getting distribution. [2] A tire company is trying to get its own franchised dealers in Europe as in America, but has had no success yet. Distribution is a special problem for replacement tires in Europe. An appliance manufacturer was considering elimination of the wholesaler link and setting up regional warehouses to permit next-day delivery after the customer chooses a model from the dealer's display. This follows an approach used in America.

Manufacturers selling to the industrial market have also extended their control over distribution upon establishing European manufacture. The first step is to have the plant act as distributor for the country where it is located. Then as volume grows and conditions permit, the pattern of company-owned distribution can be extended. In the highly competitive industrial market, technical service is one of the American manufacturer's most valuable weapons; and it is best given with controlled distribution. An equipment manufacturer said that the only place to get ahead of competition in Europe is in distribution. He added, "The first to have a controlled system of outlets will be the winner in Europe. That is the reason for Singer's success. You have to have your own outlets with trained people you can control."

Gaining greater control usually means replacing independent distributors by company personnel and organization. This poses problems in Europe as in America. Small, inefficient dealers are harder to eliminate in Europe because society and business are more protective toward them. They may have special means of survival also. A farm equipment firm said that many small "dealers," with no facilities or service, survive because they have their own "agents" selling for them, i.e., friends such as the local barber and others. A company may not need to drop all of its independent agents but may find that some of them will be a valuable nucleus to its own distribution setup. For example, a packaging firm chose its younger, more capable distributors to put on its own payroll. When it is necessary to drop independent agents, the problem is eased if they handle other lines. Their livelihood can continue through the sale of their other products and whatever new ones they can acquire. Thus, a food firm had little difficulty dropping its independent agents. However, for its long-time agents, the company gave a sort of severance pay.

Another problem arises as a firm begins to expand its ownership of distribution. When a company takes over its distribution in connection with local manufacture, the agents in other countries may become restless, wondering if they are to be dropped. Their performance may be impaired by this fear. While many manufacturers have faced similar problems in America, their foreignness in Europe accentuates the problem there.

Cooperation

For companies that are unable to gain the desired control over distribution in Europe, more efficient distribution may still be obtained through greater cooperation from intermediaries. Whereas control operates through ownership and command, cooperation derives from incentives, persuasion, and mutual benefit. In the sellers' market that prevailed in the early 1950's in Europe, the manufacturer wasn't too concerned about distributor cooperation. Today, in the very competitive buyers' market, the manufacturer--and especially the American newcomer--must obtain distributor cooperation if he is to stay in the market. Many manufacturers selling both consumer and industrial goods said that distribution was their Number One problem. Conversely, American manufacturers who have been longest in Europe consider their established distribution facilities as one of their principal advantages.

In recent years, American manufacturers have instituted many new activities and approaches in their European operations. A number of these activities have been directed toward securing distribution cooperation. Often the manufacturer will call on his American experience to help in the competitive European market.

Nondurable Goods

One method of gaining cooperation is a policy of selective distribution. This works two ways. The product line means more to the distributor because not everyone has it. The manufacturer can given more aid and attention to a smaller number of distributors. For some products, fewer distributors giving effective merchandising and service can lead to greater volume than under wide distribution where the product suffers from neglect.

Several manufacturers were using, or trying for, selective distribution in Europe. A paper goods firms was following its United States policy of "fishing where the fish are." It used its own sales force to call on important outlets with call frequency a function of volume. However, another paper goods company switched to selling through wholesalers because it felt that wide distribution was necessary for profitable volume and it couldn't cover enough retailers with its own sales force. On one product, this firm had sold only through pharmacies, the traditional European outlet for that item. When the company changed to wider distribution, it incurred the enmity of the pharmacists, who then slighted the manufacturer's whole line. The company believes that time and the evolution of European retailing are on its side, but the transition was not painless. A cosmetics manufacturer was also worried about distributor ill will in changing to widespread distribution. American experience can be useful here. While there are times when the American manufacturer should adapt to European ways, there are other times when he can bring new approaches appropriate to evolving conditions in Europe. His long-run position may be greatly strengthened if he leads the way in new distribution patterns.

There are other ways of securing distributor cooperation in Europe. Some methods used in America are applicable there, and others may arise from particular European conditions. The increase in staff and the establishment of a European headquarters and local production by American manufacturers are in themselves encouragements to distributor cooperation. The distributor now can be assured that the American manufacturer "means business" in Europe and can give special attention to local problems with on-the-spot personnel. The distributor can expect better delivery and service than in previous long-distance dealings on imports from America and thus will feel more amenable to cooperation. Wider product lines with local manufacture are an asset also.

Channels of distribution generally vary according to the nature of the product, and so do some of the ways of securing distributor cooperation. In addition to the ways already mentioned, manufacturers of consumer nondurables used heavier advertising to pre-sell their products. A soft drink company said it had increased advertising outlays and promoted the advertising to the retailers to assure shelf space in the face of growing competition. Such promotion, when accompanied by superior products, increases the value of the manufacturer's line to the retailer. Included in "superior products" are those that benefit from a particular American image and are thus more attractive to European retailers and consumers. This is the reverse of the French perfume or wine example in America.

Missionary selling or merchandising by the American manufacturers' salesmen has increased in Europe. Included in this is the supplying of point-of-purchase materials, education as to their use, and suggestions as to display. The retailer does not naively accept all this "cooperation" just to help the manufacturer, so this must be presented to him in terms of how he benefits. This involves information as to turnover and margins and explains why the task of personal selling has been intensified and upgraded (as noted in Chapter 4). A chewing gum manufacturer was faced with increasing European competition whose main weapon was lower prices. The American firm was the leader in the field and chose not to meet the lower prices but intensified its missionary selling to retailers to maintain successfully its position in the market and on distributors' shelves.

Consumer Durables and Industrial Goods

Manufacturers of consumer durables or industrial goods have used many of the techniques mentioned above, but they emphasize dealer support as they have more limited distribution. Also, the dealer's role in the sale is greater than with low-priced nondurables, which are often bought on a self-service basis. Training of distributors or their salesmen has increased. One manufacturer set up training schools in Germany, Paris, as well as one on the road for training distributors' people regarding installation of its flooring and ceiling materials. An automobile manufacturer has a business management training service for its dealers. The company expanded its distribution network in France after integration opened new opportunities. It went from eighty-five dealers in 1960 to 234 in 1963, and sales went from 2,000 vehicles to over 50,000 in the same period. It became almost impossible to find more qualified dealers, so the company set about to improve the performance of those it had by using management-training specialists.

The use of discounts or price cutting is one way to get distribution. It is not generally attractive as it is easily imitated and thus may be ineffective. It may be used by a firm with no other weapons or even by a strong firm as a last resort. A tire company was having great difficulty getting distribution in France. In desperation, it reluctantly cut prices to distributors to gain a foothold in the market. Later, it added a retread plant, which it said was partly as a service to dealers.

Offering a valuable franchise is a strong encouragement to distributor cooperation. This can apply also to nondurables, but is generally stronger with durables or industrial goods where the manufacturer's products represent an important part of the distributor's line. The value of the franchise can be both in prestige and pecuniary terms. Firms whose technical achievements are known (and promoted) around the world can be more competitive in offering franchises. This was mentioned by an electrical equipment manufacturer and others. As a good public relations gesture, one firm offered equipment and specialists to work in the Olympics. An automobile manufacturer said that much of its dealer support program was because of the need to offer a competitive franchise, i.e., to keep its present dealers and get new ones.

"Buying" Distribution

The difficulty of obtaining adequate distribution in Europe is a major reason why many firms coming relatively late in the market decided to obtain the distribution network of already established firms. This can be accomplished through acquisition, joint venture, or licensing. Several firms have used one or more of these methods. Distribution is usually carried on initially as before, but as the American firm gains experience it is usually able to add its marketing know-how to bring improvements. A firm working primarily through licensees offered extensive training and sales help for its licensees' personnel, even to supplying market studies.

As the American firm takes greater control of marketing in these ventures, the distribution methods and strategy are likely to become Americanized. If this occurs after the firm has gained experience in Europe, the more American approach will probably be suited to new conditions there. If the American approach is tried immediately by the firm without the benefit of some familiarity with Europe, the firm may be "butting its head against a stone wall." What is needed is a judicious blending of American and European experience to provide proper strategy for the "new" Europe.

There are examples of American manufacturers buying European concerns and maintaining the existing distribution system, even though the American companies already had experience plus established distribution in Europe. These acquisitions offered competitive benefits attainable no other way. A chemical firm with a small photographic film business of its own bought an established German manufacturer in this line. The American concern thus gained a larger position in the market than it could have gained in several years through its own efforts. General Electric's investment in Machines Bull and Olivetti offers similar advantages, as does Minnesota Mining and Manufacturing's purchase of Ferrania. [3]

A tire manufacturer bought a German tire producer and maintained the latter's brand and distribution in Germany in addition to its own. This gives it a dual attack on the market and gains the good will of the German brand as well. Eventually, some integration of the two will probably prove desirable. A farm equipment manufacturer faced the same situation in Italy. It said that this dual distribution and brand situation enabled it to "squeeze" competition. The company was careful, however, not to disturb mighty Fiat.

PHYSICAL DISTRIBUTION

An important step toward the realization of the Common Market lies in the formation of a common transport policy. This task was assigned to the European Commission by the Rome Treaty. The problems in transport arise because charges and conditions of carriage are nowhere determined on the basis of economic criteria, primarily or exclusively.[4] As steps toward a common transport policy are formulated and implemented, one would expect some change in the physical distribution by American manufacturers in Europe. Other factors contributing to such a change are the influence of local manufacture, a larger volume of international selling, and changed product lines. More efficient physical distribution would complement a more rational distribution strategy and mean greater benefit to manufacturer and consumer alike.

At the time of this study, there had been little progress in the EEC toward a common transport policy. In June, 1965, the EEC Council of Ministers did reach agreement on a common system for organizing the transport market. However, implementation is quite another matter. Thus, it is not surprising that there has been little change in the transportation practices of American manufacturers in Europe. Changes have naturally occurred in conjunction with local manufacture or rationalization of production, but the new practices must continue to consider national differences in transport policy. There has been greater coordination of transport as well as of distribution in connection with establishment of European headquarters, but local peculiarities still interfer with uniform practice. For example, a food firm sells to most of the EEC through its Swiss sales subsidiary. Production is in Italy. Shipping to Belgium, the company uses the French National Railways favored by the French government. To Hamburg, Germany, the company uses river and canal transport. The railroad rates are the same, but there is more favorable customs treatment with the use of waterways.

Several firms are studying their transport problems in
Europe to be able to coordinate in view of the eventual realization of the customs union and a common transport policy.
There is also the desire for more efficient current operations. Some have traffic departments at European headquarters
coordinating physical distribution for Europe. After study
of its distribution, one company reduced the number of its
warehouses to obtain more strategic branch marketing. It
also is switching to greater use of trucks rather than trains.
The respondent noted: "We are emphasizing strategic marketing rather than mere physical supply as we did with exports."

The problems of physical distribution deserve continued
attention by American manufacturers in Europe. It appears,
however, that significant changes will depend on much greater
progress toward a common transport policy--or technological
innovation.

CONCLUSIONS

Internationalizing of Distribution

Distribution channels in the Common Market are almost
exclusively national, even when production is centralized.
Though the logic of a common market implies a rationalizing
of distribution patterns disregarding political boundaries, this
has not yet happened in the EEC. Strong historical and cultural
differences between Member Countries mean that distribution networks will be national for several years to come. Nevertheless, there are a few preliminary steps toward greater
international distribution by those companies who are anticipating the Europe of tomorrow.

Increased Control and Cooperation
in Distribution

In connection with their increased activity in Europe,
American manufacturers have increased their control over
distribution. This has meant more direct channels, with the
manufacturer taking over more of the distribution task himself. American companies have also worked hard to secure
greater cooperation from independent intermediaries. For
this, the manufacturers have used the same tools they use

in America plus a few others especially applicable to Europe.
Some American firms newer in the market have had to "buy"
distribution to gain an entry in the market. This has been
done through acquisition, joint venture, or licensing.

Physical Distribution

Though the Rome Treaty envisions a common transportation policy for the EEC, little progress has been made toward
its realization. Continuing differences in regulations and
policies of the Member Countries have prevented major changes
in physical distribution in the Common Market.

NOTES TO CHAPTER 5

1. James B. Jefferys and Derek Knee, Retailing in Europe;
Present Structure and Future Trends (London: Macmillan
& Co., Ltd., 1962), pp. 1-177.

2. "Comment Chrysler a refait la distance," Enterprise,
No. 455 (May 30, 1964), 33ff.

3. "Europe's Photographic Industry," The Economist,
CCXI, 6303 (June 13, 1964), 1266.

4. J. E. Meade, H. H. Liesner, and S. J. Wells, Case
Studies in Economic Union (London: Oxford University Press,
1962), p. 403.

CHAPTER **6** PRICING

The words "pricing policy" imply that the manufacturer has some control over the prices at which he sells his products. The fact that the producer's knowledge of his marginal costs and marginal revenues is incomplete, the existence of imperfect competition with varying degrees of product differentiation, and the presence of monopolistic elements in supply all mean that pricing becomes a matter of marketing strategy rather than merely accepting the dictum of the market. In his approach to the EEC, an American manufacturer must, therefore, consider price as one element of his marketing program on which decisions and adjustments will have to be made.

The development of the Common Market and other changes occurring in Europe suggest an adjustment in the pricing practices of American manufacturers as part of their over-all adaptation to the EEC. The opening of the Common Market should mean not only greater competition but more emphasis on price as a competitive weapon. The greater emphasis on, and investment in, the EEC should lead to a more distinctly European pricing policy by American manufacturers. The growth of unification in the EEC should encourage and facilitate uniform market-wide pricing in place of diverse national practices.

INCREASED PRICE COMPETITION

In classical economics, competition and price competition were generally synonymous. In more recent decades, and especially in the work of Edward Chamberlin, different forms of nonprice competition were formally recognized. In his study of the theory of economic integration, Balassa concludes that integration will be conducive to both price competition and nonprice competition. [1] One would expect American firms to be leaders in price competition in view of their domestic experience and the conservative European practice and price agreements. [2]

Price competition has increased in the EEC since 1957, according to the experience of three fourths of the respondent companies. The pressure of price competition was noted especially by manufacturers of consumer durables and industrial goods. There are many reasons for this increased price sensitivity in Europe. European recovery from World War II led to reestablishment of supply capability and eventually to a buyers' market with consequent pressure on prices. Economic integration opened national markets to new competitors and encouraged many to expand production facilities. This expansion led in many cases to excess capacity, especially in consumer durables and industrial goods where there were greater opportunities for international selling. Several respondents noted this problem of excess capacity, and some said it was because European firms were less likely to do market research before expanding plant. On the other hand, some American manufacturers admitted that they also had overbuilt because of insufficient preparatory research.

Another reason for pressure on prices is the lower degree of profit consciousness of many European manufacturers. While profit maximization is not the only, or necessarily major, goal of American manufacturers (Fortune's prestigious "500" ranking is on sales volume), profits are usually a greater concern to them than to European manufacturers. For Europeans, social concerns (and even personal concerns in the case of family firms) often outweigh profit considerations. For example, the desire to maintain employment or exports may lead to price cutting and lower profits. This lower degree of profit consciousness is especially notable in government-owned European firms, such as Renault in France. The government's desire to earn foreign exchange and maintain employment is much greater than its need for a little extra money in the treasury. American manufacturers, however, run their European subsidiaries as profit centers and usually resent the price pressure from such European competitors. For example, one automobile executive expressed such sentiments and said American competitors were "more sensible."

A further reason for increased price competition is that many European competitors breaking into new lines or new markets have no other competitive weapon than a lower price. Firms that are large and well entrenched emphasize promotion, distribution, service, or other forms of nonprice com-

petition   and may even collaborate to divide up markets and
restrict new entrants.   However, many European firms, unable to mount a big promotional campaign, rely on a low
price to break into a market.   The larger American companies
usually rely on nonprice methods.   As a leading German in-
dustrialist noted,   "To date, the Americans have used no com-
bative prices.   They try to win the market most of all with
intensive advertising campaigns."[3]   Some American manufacturers, however, have used the same list price to consumers as their competitors, but then have given bigger discounts to distributors.   Others admitted to selling at a loss
occasionally as a holding action.   These firms could not afford to lose their foothold in the market--or, in some cases
their dealer organizations.   They viewed the price cutting as
a necessary, but temporary, strategy.

American Firms Not Price Leaders

As implied in the preceding paragraph, the American
firms have not generally been leaders in competing on a price
basis in Europe.   While price competition is probably greater
in America, and pricing agreements more common in Europe,
the increased price competition in Europe owes more to factors mentioned above than to the presence of American manufacturers.   Practically all respondents mentioned the need
to "be competitive" in prices, but very few American companies tried to lead in price cutting.   Most felt that the edge
obtained by price cutting was apt to be short-lived and unprofitable and, therefore, emphasized various forms of nonprice
competition to gain a more enduring advantage.

Nonprice Competition

Product quality and distinctiveness were claimed by many
as a reason for not selling at the lowest price.   A durable
goods company said it had to cut prices where quality was
similar but could get a premium price where it had a superior
product.   A packaging company said there was excess capacity
in the industry but that the firm was differentiating its products to avoid direct price competition.   American chemical
companies let European competitors take over production of
many staple items and then turned to specialty products where
price competition was less.

Various types of service (both pre-sale and post-sale) were used by American manufacturers to minimize price competition. Some consumer nondurables firms used missionary selling to distributors instead of price cuts, but service was emphasized most by manufacturers of durables and industrial goods. Enlarged staffs of product specialists and more high quality sales-service personnel have enabled many American manufacturers to maintain or expand their positions against competitors whose only weapon is price. An American chemical firm even noted that it sometimes had a higher price on some standard products because of the extensive services it offered, both before and after the sale.

Advertising, another type of nonprice competition, is generally more heavily used by American firms than by their European competitors. A notable example of this is Proctor and Gamble's successful entry into France (cited in Chapter 4, "Promotion").

Resale price maintenance was used by about half of the consumer goods firms in one or more Member Countries. This is a further indication of their emphasis on nonprice forms of competition. While the practice of resale price maintenance is gradually fading in Europe (and is not generally allowed in France), many American manufacturers will use it in certain markets if it is industry practice, as they are happy to compete in other ways. Because the European situation seems to be following American experience with "Fair Trade," one company sent a marketing executive to inform subsidiaries of what had happened in America. Thus, they would know the factors affecting the company's interests in the issue and be ready for the similar conflict coming in Europe on resale price maintenance.

There were a few exceptions to the general rule that American firms aren't "price-cutters" in Europe. A tire company had to cut prices to distributors in France after it failed to get distribution any other way. An automobile manufacturer had to cut price to break into the Italian market with imported cars. To sell at a competitive price and allow the standard dealer margin, the company had to start with rather unprofitable sales. One consumer goods firm had trouble breaking into the European market because its leading competitor (another American firm) was practicing a "stay out" pricing policy to prevent entry of competitors.

ADAPTATION OF PRICING
TO EUROPEAN REQUIREMENTS

As part of their adjustment to the European market, American manufacturers have adapted their pricing practices to European conditions. In many cases, however, this adaptation was not related to the development of the Common Market but occurred when the companies established European production. Nevertheless, the EEC did play a role here in encouraging other American manufacturers to initiate or expand European operations and to pay closer attention to all aspects of these operations, including pricing. Increasing competition and development of a buyers' market in Europe accentuated the need for "European" pricing.

Establishment of European manufacture is the principal occasion when pricing is adapted to Europe. Thereafter, the American manufacturers' European prices tend to be determined by European demand and supply conditions. With exports, the prices are generally determined by supply and demand conditions in America.

The opening of manufacturing subsidiaries or European headquarters frequently means a decentralizing of pricing authority to Europe. The subsidiaries, when operating as profit centers, need a large degree of authority over price. In spite of this decentralization, there is often an increase in parent-company attention to European prices. This may result from the company's greater interest in European business or from a need to coordinate prices when there are several national production centers in the integrated market. In the latter case, the subsidiaries may have autonomy in pricing for their national market, but be controlled in their export pricing.

It should also be noted that adaptation of product is frequently the equivalent of adaptation of price. The automobiles and refrigerators produced by American manufacturers in Europe are smaller--and cheaper. Both crackers and facial tissues come in smaller packages in Europe--to get a lower shelf price.

Three examples illustrate some of the problems in adapting price. A consumer goods firm was exporting a product to one market where it retailed at 100 lire. With local production, the product could retail at 70 lire and enjoy an expanded market. However, the retailers preferred the old price of 100 lire. The company considered advertising the 70 lire price to consumers but feared incurring the ill will of retailers and losing distribution. Instead, it subsidized a number of key retailers to sell at the new low price and successfully broke the "price barrier."

Drug pricing represents an example of the role of government in forcing adaptation. American drug manufacturers selling in Europe have little choice about adapting prices. On many of their products, a meticulous price justification must be made before government medical boards. The result is government-controlled prices. One respondent noted that most European countries with government medical-care schemes are underfunded in their medical programs as the governments underestimated the increase in the use of medical services with socialized medicine. This brings price pressure on the manufacturer as great as that from increased competition.

A manufacturer of convenience foods shows the influence of the customs union on price as well as the problem of pricing to break into the market. The company has one production source for the whole EEC. Anticipating the elimination of internal tariffs, the company already prices assuming zero tariffs when selling through its EEC sales subsidiary. The company absorbs the loss to the extent that tariffs still exist. This means that it raises the price to national distributors each time the internal tariffs drop, as the distributor pays the tariff. The distributor's net price remains the same, however. The company, which is quite new in Europe, sets prices on expected "optimal" volume attainable a few years hence rather than on present low volume.

Thus, the company is testing market acceptance at the price it expects to have when the customs union is fully realized and adequate volume is attained. It is willing to take losses to get established in the market. However, the company has not adapted one aspect of its pricing policy. It offers no quantity discounts in Europe or America. In

America, it has been able to maintain this position because
of the dominance of its brand. In Europe, however, its brand
is not well-established and there is a question as to how rigidly
it can maintain this policy in view of the growth of corporate
and voluntary chains and the company's need to get a stronger
market position. Adaptation would seem to be the wiser course
here, with pricing practice determined by the European competitive situation rather than the American.

TRENDS IN UNIFORM MARKET-
WIDE PRICING PRACTICE

There are many reasons why one would expect American
manufacturers to be using more uniform market-wide pricing in the EEC. First, there is the formation of the customs
union, which has made important strides in cutting tariffs and
reducing other barriers to trade. The EEC program for harmonizing diverse national regulations affecting trade should
help the customs union become more of a common market.
These two factors along with others have led to a great increase
in international selling and a consequent need for more unified
pricing practice. Related to this is the increase in specialization of production (i. e. , plants producing products for the
whole market), which facilitates more uniform pricing. Finally, their domestic experience and their desire for a "clean-
er, " more manageable pricing system would lead American
manufacturers to unify pricing practices where possible.

Pressures for Pricing Diversity

Contrary to expectation, there has not been a great increase in the uniformity of American manufacturers' pricing practices in the Common Market. Some have taken
steps toward uniformity, but with others pricing practices
have become less standardized than before. While their
pricing policies for each Member Country are very similar,
if not identical, American manufacturers' pricing practices
often vary from country to country. The above-mentioned
pressures for uniformity are less strong than other pressures causing diversity of prices and pricing.

The establishment of European production in one or more
countries has often led to greater diversity in pricing, especially if plants produce for national markets. American

export prices are generally based on the price and supply and demand conditions in America with little consideration for European requirements. Products manufactured locally are usually adapted in price as well as other product characteristics. As indicated in Chapter 3, "Product Policy," this adaptation often varies from country to country so that firms that changed to local production from exports probably have more diversity in European pricing than before. If production is national, then production costs will differ from country to country also.

Even if production is specialized in the EEC, with each plant producing products for the whole market, the existence of national marketing subsidiaries or the use of a different marketing mix in each Member Country means that pricing will tend to vary by country.

Where national subsidiaries are profit centers, they will have an important, if not controlling, voice in setting price. Prices are thus set by different people in different countries according to different conditions and profit goals. While this activity is subject to parent-company control, there may or may not be coordination of it. An example of differences between subsidiaries is the drug firm that had one product that it was selling for $3. 25 per unit in Belgium and $2. 40 for the same unit in France. The company was well-established in Belgium but was trying to introduce the new product into the competitive French market. The French subsidiary manager saw the possibility of the French government buying from "drug pirates" in Italy. His lower price was approved by the parent company to enable him to meet this threat in France.

Sometimes in joint ventures or acquisitions, the Americans will leave pricing largely to the European managers, who have greater market experience. Each joint venture or acquisition may follow its previous national pattern with little international standardization or pricing practice by the American company, except for export sales.

The major pricing guideline mentioned by almost all the respondents was the need to be competitive locally. Though international selling has greatly increased in the Common Market, for many products the national markets are dominated

by national producers; and the competitive situation varies by
country. While the American manufacturer finds regional
competitive differences domestically, the differences in
Europe are greater. For example, a manufacturer of business machines claimed to have uniform pricing throughout
Europe. However, when Germany and the Netherlands re-
valued their currencies by 5 per cent, the company cut
its prices 5 per cent in the Netherlands, but not in Germany,
because of differing competitive conditions. Competition
varies not only by country but by product. Thus, a company may plan for 3 per cent profit margin on product
"A" and 15 per cent margin on product "L" where it has
little competition. In another country, these margins might
be reversed.

In addition to the organizational and marketing reasons
for pricing diversity, there are many uncommon factors in
the EEC environment. There is not uniformity of pricing in
the Common Market because market conditions frequently
do not permit it. The different governmental regulations affecting trade have yet to be harmonized. The example of
drug companies having to meet price requirements of different national medical boards has already been cited. Automobile manufacturers must be sensitive to the differing national taxes on their products. Firms that use resale-price
maintenance find national diversity in this--though the whole
practice of resale-price maintenance is disappearing in the
EEC. A special and uniquely national governmental pricing
regulation was the French "freeze" on prices that began in
1963 and continued into 1966.

The fact of differing national currencies affects pricing
practice, especially where a "convenient" price is sought
(such as a nickel or dime in the United States). If the product is standardized and the actual coins or currency units
in use in each country differ in value, uniform pricing is difficult. While manufacturers of such products as soft drinks
or chewing gum are more concerned about this, a uniform
currency would reduce the pricing problems of all producers
selling internationally.

Partly a question of taxes, but also a function of distribution channels and discount structures, is the whole matter of
"add-ons" to the factory or import price. It isn't rare for

products to follow different distribution channels in different
countries, and this means different pricing systems. Even if
channels are the same, the discount and tax structures vary
importantly between Member Countries and complicate the
pricing problem. Though the basic price to distributors in
different countries may be identical, the manufacturer is even
more concerned with the consumer price since the acceptance
and penetration of his product depend primarily on that.

An example from the consumer nondurables area illustrates the complexity and variety of "add-ons." A manufacturer was selling into France and Germany at the same
price to the importer-distributor. The "add-ons," however,
varied as follows:

	Duty	Transmission Tax	Importer	Wholesale Margin	Retail Margin
France	3%	25%	12%	15%	31%
Germany	12%	6%	23%	12.5%	20%

Steps Toward Pricing Uniformity

Though various market and governmental factors cause
variety in prices and pricing practice, American manufacturers try to realize the highest degree of uniformity currently
possible. Centralization of pricing authority is almost essential for pricing coordination or uniformity. This authority may be centralized in Europe or America. If there is
one production source for Europe, the pricing problem is
simplified, whether that source be American exports or European production. Where the firm has several production
sources for Europe, conflict may arise between the goals
of various profit centers and over-all corporate goals.

If European operations are self-contained on both the
supply and demand sides, a strong argument can be made
for centralizing pricing authority at European headquarters.
If the company's products are coming partly from non-European sources or going to non-European markets, it is more
reasonable to centralize pricing authority in America. This
is the most frequent practice (when there is centralized pricing authority). Problems of intracountry pricing enter in
also. Because of tariffs, national taxes, or other reasons,

companies will want to vary the country in which they receive
their greatest profit. However, governments, both foreign and
American, also have something to say about such transfer
prices.

The largest companies with the greatest diversity in possible product sources generally have the most centralized pricing authority, as well as the greatest need for it. Each company handles it somewhat differently. One firm has its finance
committee justify pricing and product allocation initially, and
then the marketing people look at the price from the viewpoint
of competition and other market factors. This company has no
formula for pricing but works on it on this ad hoc basis.
Another firm uses a standardized billing price for products
from three or four sources. While price to the buyer in any
European country is the same from each source, production
costs vary; and the allocation of orders is often decided
centrally rather than by the marketing subsidiary in the purchasing country. A Business International study covers in
some detail such general international pricing problems. [4]

CONCLUSIONS

Price competition has increased in the Common Market
as expected, but American manufacturers have played a
much smaller role in this than one would think. American
companies have used their great financial and research resources to emphasize product differentiation, promotion, and
other nonprice competition. European manufacturers faced
with new competitors and excess capacity have been the generally reluctant causes of increased price competition.

The expected increase in more distinctly European pricing did occur. The establishment of local manufacture and
the new interest in European business by American companies
were the principal reasons. Firms long established in Europe, however, had adapted their pricing practices to local requirements already before the Common Market.

The anticipated rise in the uniformity of American manufacturers' pricing practices in the Common Market was not
much in evidence. The principal reasons were that government regulations and other differences in national markets
did not permit or warrant a unified pricing practice.

The proper pricing strategy for an American manufacturer in Europe will depend on the position and goals of the particular firm. To find the right approach, however, requires careful study because the relevant variables are changing faster in Europe than in America. Some firms are conducting special research on factors affecting pricing and distribution so as to be ready for the full customs union, which will soon be realized. While some centralized control and coordination is needed, a strong degree of decentralization may be desired (where possible) in line with local profit responsibilities. Decentralization helps to assure maximum use of local knowledge and to gain the necessary flexibility. Some firms found that a rigid pricing policy by executives in America hindered their maneuverability in European operations. Some executives seem to feel that what is good for America is good for the rest of the world. The European market, however, is important enough to deserve special attention.

The important thing to note is that changes are occurring and will continue to occur--in taxes, tariffs, resale-price maintenance, harmonization of laws, and other variables affecting pricing. American experience will help an American manufacturer to plot his course. However, this American experience must be modified by experience and careful study in Europe itself.

NOTES TO CHAPTER 6

1. Bela Balassa, The Theory of Economic Integration (Homewood, Ill. : Richard D. Irwin, Inc. , 1961), pp. 163-67.

2. Tibor Scitovsky, Economic Theory and Western European Integration (Stanford, Calif. : Stanford University Press, 1958), p. 27.

3. "Hard-Driving Americans Push Small Firms to the Wall, " German International, VI, 4 (April 30, 1962), 20.

4. Solving International Pricing Problems (New York: Business International, 1965), pp. 1-50.

CHAPTER **7** MARKETING
RESEARCH

Previous chapters have discussed the need for various
types of adjustments for successful marketing in the EEC.
Marketing research is an indispensable tool for determining
the nature and extent of these adjustments. Marketing research in the present discussion will be used in the broad
sense to include investigation of market and economic factors,
competition, distribution, and consumer reaction to products
or advertising appeals.[1] Thus, the definition includes that
research that helps a manufacturer make the right decisions
about investments and the choice of products, promotion,
and distribution for the Common Market.

Marketing research has enjoyed growing acceptance in
America since World War II; but in Europe, until recent
years, American manufacturers were enjoying a sellers' market and often taking a rather casual, passive approach to European business. Since the mid-1950's the European situation
has radically changed: European productive capacity is restored, its technological sophistication is close to America's,
wealth has been increased and democratized, and economic
integration is changing the psychology of the Old World. These
changes have drawn American manufacturers to participate
more actively in Europe and also made their task more difficult. While there are certain parallels between the European and American economies, only a rash manufacturer would
undertake European operations without a careful study of the
crucial differences. Marketing research is probably more
important to the American manufacturer in Europe than in his
domestic operations, where he has a wealth of experience.
Furthermore, changes in competitive conditions and consumer habits are occurring at a faster pace in Europe. Nevertheless, many American companies have gone in with insufficient knowledge and consideration of European peculiarities.[2]

European manufacturers have greatly increased their use
of marketing research since the opening of the Common Market.[3]

Such research has an element of both offensive and defensive strategy. American manufacturers have also initiated or greatly expanded their use of marketing research in Europe since 1957. While they are often leaders in the use of this tool in Europe, many have resorted to it only after unfortunate experiences in the market. They have learned by experience, which is still the best teacher, though its lessons are costly. Marketing research is usually much cheaper than a reverse in the market.

GROWING ROLE OF
MARKETING RESEARCH

Market and Marketing Factors

Many variables have affected the role of marketing research in the European operations of American manufacturers. The investment required with local production caused many to "look" at the market carefully before "leaping" across the ocean. Others, because of previous experience with exports, felt they knew the market when they established local manufacture. However, the marketing situation, product line, and distribution may well be different with local production. A rubber company, which had been exporting to France, set up a French plant with the same production "ticket" as the export product line. It turned out that these products were replacement tires for American cars, which were of diminishing significance in the new European market. Costly production-line adjustments were necessary. The experience led to the hiring of a professional marketing researcher for international operations. Before another plant was opened in Italy, this researcher did an on-the-spot, five-week study of the market. A chemical company was more cautious in beginning European production. It has twelve new plants in Europe and before placing each one it conducted market studies, including the question as to which economic unit--EEC or EFTA--had the largest "domestic" market for the plant's products.

Careful study is needed before investment in European manufacture. It is likewise essential before undertaking other changes in European operations. Before entering a new market, with or without local manufacture, research can bring to light some of the threats and opportunities present. A soft drink manufacturer studies not only consumer tastes and habits, but also the food, packaging, and promotional regulations before entering new countries. A drug firm hired consultants to do a detailed study of the German market. However, a women's clothing company merely visited major department stores before starting to sell in Germany and France. A manufacturer of flooring materials built a plant in Germany without sufficient market research and found itself in a market characterized by excess capacity and low prices. It is holding on but is dissatisfied with the profit picture.

New-product introduction is another major undertaking where manufacturers have a need for market analysis. In view of the great cost of product development and introduction, the relatively small cost of marketing research seems like inexpensive insurance to help avoid failures. A farm equipment manufacturer has learned this well and requires market analysis before approving development work on any new product idea. A packaging firm added marketing research personnel to its European product-design department. It tests the packages to be able to offer the customer one with proven consumer acceptance. A consumer goods firm added marketing research activities after its attempted introduction of a leading American product it felt was "right" for Europe. After the expensive campaign failed, the company found that consumers had other ideas about the "right" product. The products were changed to conform with market desires.

Establishment of European manufacture, greater international selling, and changing patterns of retailing can all require adjustments in the European distribution of American manufacturers. When the manufacturer wants to adapt his distribution pattern to the new situation, he can again be guided by research findings. A paper goods producer had consultants do a market survey before introducing one of its leading consumer products into France. A year later it conducted another study before changing from selective to mass distribution of the product. For this firm, as for most, American experience was valuable in marketing to Europe. However, the relevance of this experience depends on various European or national peculiarities that can be determined only by local marketing research.

European integration brought its own changes and accelerated others that caused American companies to step up their
market analysis to gain guidance in the new environment. The
buyers' market, discretionary income, and increased competition were mentioned by several companies as reasons for their
increased marketing research activity. One respondent remarked that such research was relatively less important than
in America as the company's sales were growing faster on the
Continent. Nevertheless, the company had extensive marketing
research activity in its European subsidiaries.

European sales volume was an important variable affecting
the amount of marketing research done by some American
companies. Several mentioned that they could use more market analysis but couldn't afford it on present volume. This
is analogous to setting advertising appropriations as a percen-
tage of sales. It depends on the firm's market goals and particular situation, but it would seem that marketing research
is not the best place to economize if the firm has the capacity
to get a larger market share. Of course, if research has re-
vealed certain problems in the path of increased sales, these
should probably be resolved first.

Organizational Factors

Besides the above reasons that have encouraged an expanded American use of marketing research in Europe, there
are organizational factors leading to the same result. As
part of company development, many firms have increased
their marketing research activity in domestic operations.
This has often carried over to the international side, especially in firms that have a large per cent of their business overseas and endeavor to coordinate the two operations. A food
manufacturer and a soft drink company are good examples
of this type of growth in use of market analysis. In one European division, a change of top-level personnel resulted in new
management approaches and a big increase in the use of marketing research.

A more common organizational factor is company reorganization for international business. This is usually accompanied by higher goals in Europe and caused several companies to add a marketing research activity. (Examples have
already been given of firms that did not include this activity

in their international reorganization, but added it after reverses
in the market.) This new activity may be in the American or
European headquarters, or both. Frequently, there is a decentralization of this activity to Europe, though with some kind
of control from America. A consumer goods firm sent a vice-
president to reorganize its European operations during a three-
year stay at its headquarters in London. His first action was
to hire a marketing research expert. He noted: "Before we
were going by the seat of our pants. We really had no information on which to base decisions." Many have located their
marketing research staff in Switzerland; but others are found
at European headquarters in Brussels, Paris, Rome, or London.

Occasionally, a firm's special knowledge of its own product area and its experience in the market meant that a lesser
need was felt for marketing research. This was more likely
when the firm was a leader in its product line and had years
of experience in the European market. While these firms invariably were carrying on market research, some felt their
own experience and knowledge to be more valuable. A vice-
president who had headed his firm's European operations for
many years said, "The company knows a lot about its job.
I don't like this modern 'hocus pocus.' We have found that
there isn't much variation from country to country for our
product." (The product was a consumer good that the firm
had introduced into Europe.) Other firms in somewhat similar positions, however, felt that rapidly changing conditions
required special new knowledge such as could be obtained best
through marketing research.

CONDUCT OF MARKETING RESEARCH

American manufacturers' marketing research activities in
Europe have increased greatly in recent years, but there are
different ways in which this research is carried on. The research itself must generally be done in Europe, of course, but
there are varying degrees of control from America. Within
Europe, the research may be conducted by subsidiaries, European headquarters, the company's advertising agency, or
special research groups, or a combination of these.

Control from America

In accord with the decentralizing tendencies in many aspects of international business, the marketing research staff is
increasingly located in Europe. This is desirable since the
market is there, and even modern air travel doesn't permit
this type of work to be handled on a commuter basis. In spite
of this decentralization, there is a lot of attention and control
from America, in line with the new corporate interest in European business. The responsible person in the international
division may be the marketing manager, director of marketing research, or assistant vice-president--marketing. One
director of marketing research prepares a complete study
design before getting bids from European firms for the job.
He did a personal five-week study in one Member Country
before the company built a plant there. Firms selling to the
industrial market also sent United States personnel over to
do studies. A product specialist in Europe for a new-product
introduction carried out a market survey during his stay.
Other companies send United States experts on a consultant
basis.

Conduct of marketing research by personnel from
America is not the rule, however. Most frequently, personnel in Europe will undertake the studies under the direction or surveillance of American staff or executives. This
type of decentralization allows area specialization by those
familiar with the market while permitting some long-distance
coordination and contribution from the American experts.
One consumer goods firm coordinates through its United
States marketing research staff and semiannual coordinating meetings with subsidiaries. It also sends them copies
of studies done in the United States. Another firm hires out
most of its work in Europe, but the impetus and control are
by the international marketing executive. This man felt the
Europeans were weak in this area and expected to retain tight
control for some time. A respondent in the industrial market shared this opinion and said the first task of their Americans doing marketing research in Europe is to train a national. This company did no such research five years ago. Now
it has a specialist in each operating group and coordinates
and guides through its world director of marketing and economic research.

The Actual Research in Europe

Who conducts the actual research in Europe depends on
the size and nature of the company's operation there and the
organization and philosophy of the firm. Rephrasing Adam
Smith, one could say, "Specialization is limited by the size
of the business." Companies with large, wholly owned, multi-
million-dollar operations in Europe can afford (and probably
need) in-house marketing research activity. Companies who
make extensive use of this tool in America and who have
quite a degree of decentralization to Europe are likely to have
such an in-house research staff in Europe.

Several of the largest companies had a marketing research
activity at each major subsidiary, which is almost always a
producing subsidiary rather than one with just sales responsibility. One of the largest firms had a marketing research
group in each of eight major European countries as well as
at European headquarters in Paris (a staff of sixteen) and
at international headquarters in New York (staff of forty-four).
This industrial marketer has sales of several hundred million
dollars in Europe. A durables manufacturer had four groups:
one each with its EEC and EFTA plants, one in Brussels for the
European countries where it had only sales subsidiaries, and
one at American headquarters. A food firm had each affiliate
doing its own marketing studies, with the specialist at Swiss
headquarters helping to train in the latest techniques.

Firms with modest European sales can't afford full-time
marketing research groups in each subsidiary. Nevertheless,
these subsidiaries will need market information as much as
those of the largest firms. One way to meet this need is to
establish one qualified group for the whole EEC or all of
Europe. This is done frequently at European headquarters.
One consumer goods company began a marketing research
group at its London headquarters in 1959. The vice-president
who started this explained, "We're centralizing our 'mr' to
have one good department rather than ten 'half-baked' operations. It operates on a service basis to all our European
companies." A cosmetic firm works in the same way.

Some manufacturers in the industrial market operate in
a similar fashion even though sales are quite large. Because
they do more international selling on an industry basis, cen-

tralized marketing studies can be more meaningful than in consumer goods, where national differences are important.   Again,
these centralized groups are usually at European headquarters.
With some chemical companies, the sales-service people or
product specialists conduct their own market research in the
course of their intimate contact with the consumer's business.
The European headquarters then pulls it all together.   This
is done on an individual product basis generally.   An electrical
equipment firm also uses its product specialists for market
studies.

Companies that can't afford a full marketing research
staff even at European headquarters have other ways of meeting their market information needs.   They may have one man
with the subsidiaries or at headquarters and hire out the
studies they require.   A soft drink marketer had an expert
in Rome and hired national agencies in the country where the
study was to be done.   Many companies with their own personnel will frequently hire out special studies.   They may need
specialized help on a particular study, or they may have staffing
problems.   A drug manufacturer used its own staff for regular
needs and hired outside agencies to meet extra demands.
Some marketers mentioned that the need to educate an outside agency about the firm and its industry was a factor limiting their use.

Firms operating through joint ventures or licensees have
less control over the conduct of marketing research.   Where
the European partner is a sophisticated marketer, this research
can be left to it, with occasional American contributions.   This
was the policy of a firm associated with Unilever in one venture.
In other cases, marketing know-how may be a major contribution of the American partner, as was the case with one paper
goods producer joined with a raw materials supplier.   Licensors
can generally expect little marketing research from their
licensees even though both would benefit.   In such cases, the
licensor may have to carry the whole burden and hope for a
payoff in good will and increased royalties.   One major licensor makes available to its licensees   all of its marketing
studies that   are pertinent to the licensee's business.

Various agencies are available to do marketing research
in Europe.   There are European marketing research groups
and advertising agencies, plus American companies in the

same fields. Advertising agency departments are often called
on for market research and, in any case, frequently do research in connection with advertising campaigns. European
agencies are favored by some manufacturers and are being
called on more as they grow in experience and competence;
whichever agency is chosen, it will almost invariably be located in Europe. One exception was for a lengthy study of a
firm's total European operations and markets. This was done
at the advent of the Common Market and resulted in a profitable reorganization for doing business in an integrated Europe.
The veteran international firm hired an American research
institute for this job.

Opinions differ as to the quality of European marketing
research. Some were dissatisfied with work done, and one
firm had to repeat a study with a second agency. Others
felt that some European groups were as good as American.
The training role of marketing-oriented American firms
and advertising agencies and the growing interest in marketing by Europeans themselves have been forces increasing
the quantity and quality of European marketing research.
Of course, such European firms as Unilever and Nestle have
always been au courant.

A supplementary source of marketing information is the
general studies done by American or European consultant
groups. Some food marketers purchased an Arthur D.
Little study of food marketing in Europe. Others used
material from the Economist Intelligence Unit on various
national markets.

Information for European marketing is thus available from
many company and noncompany sources. It has a price; but,
like life insurance, it is something the prudent man will not
do without--the amount of coverage depending on particular
circumstances.

The American manufacturer who wants a profitable share
of European business will have to adapt his marketing activities
in Europe. Only with good market information can the proper
adaptations be made. Marketing research is the manufacturer's intelligence tool to help him survive and succeed in the
"new" Europe. Its importance has been demonstrated by the
experience of the American firms recounted in this chapter.

NOTES TO CHAPTER 7

1. A. B. Blankenship, "Needed: A Broader Concept of Marketing Research," Journal of Marketing, XIII, 3 (January, 1949), 305-10.

2. "World Business," Time, LXXXIV, 8 (August 21, 1964), 82.

3. Marketing Science Institute, Marketing Development in the European Economic Community (New York: McGraw-Hill Book Co., Inc., 1964), p. 102.

CHAPTER 8   THE COMPETITIVE SITUATION

As Scitovsky has noted, restraints on international trade are restraints on competition. [1] As trade is freed between Member Countries in the EEC, one would expect an increase in competition in the Common Market. Producers who sold primarily to their national market before can now sell to other Member Countries. Since the stronger, more aggressive firms are the first to go international, there would be an increase in the quality as well as the quantity of competition.

The reestablishment of Europe's supply capability should further increase competition. In the first postwar decade, European manufacturers were reconstructing plant and operating in a sellers' market. As European recovery progressed, capacity was restored and a buyers' market gradually developed. A third pressure for increased competition in the EEC is the wave of new investment by American manufacturers. This increases the supply potential and competitive pressure. Finally, the new "Rules of Competition" in the Rome Treaty should contribute to making Europe more competitive than previously.

Although they are often relatively unfamiliar with Europe and face strong competition there, American manufacturers should enjoy certain competitive advantages enabling them to realize some success in the EEC. Their American operations have given them valuable experience both in mass production and mass marketing. In the integrated Common Market, this experience should stand them in good stead. The generally high consumer orientation of American manufacturers should give them an edge in the EEC, where a buyers' market prevails and consumption is being democratized. Furthermore, American manufacturers frequently enjoy greater financial resources than their European competitors.

INCREASED COMPETITION IN THE EEC

Sources of the New Competition

The respondents were unanimous in finding that the competitive situation in Member Countries is tougher now than before the formation of the Common Market. Even though demand has been rising quite steadily over the years, it is now more difficult for the American manufacturer to establish or maintain a position in the market. The study covered just the years since the signing of the Rome Treaty, but it would be misleading to credit the development of the Common Market as the sole, or necessarily major, source of the increased competition.

The major single source of the increase in competition has been the renewed strength of European producers. Their resurgence is both a cause and effect of European recovery and began well before 1958. American aid was a factor in the reconstruction of European manufacturing, but European producers reached a "take-off" stage of self-sustaining growth during the 1950's. The stronger cord of European competitiveness is composed of several strands: Plants are rebuilt and modernized; financial resources are generally strong; research and development activity is extensive; mergers have given strength through unity (and here the Common Market was a contributing factor); European manufacturers have become more sophisticated marketers. In the upgrading of European marketing, the example of American manufacturers, the presence of American advertising agencies, and the pressure of a buyers' market have all had an influence.

A second source of increased competition in the Member Countries has been the growth of international selling. While the restoration of European productive capacity was necessary for this, it was the formation of the customs union that gave the greatest impetus to producers to sell in other Member Countries. Firms that had a comfortable niche in their own national market (perhaps assured by an agreement between producers) found the Common Market opening the doors to new "foreign" competitors. In each national market, the number of sellers increased relatively more than the number of buyers--or their purchasing power. Of course, it was this threat (or promise) of the Common Market that caused many mergers or joint undertakings, both within countries and across national boundaries. These mergers often strengthened competition, though reducing the number of competitors.

A third source of increased competition has been the entry of firms from outside the EEC. New or expanded activity of American manufacturers has been the major foreign element. However, several respondents mentioned strong competition from the English in chemicals and automobiles; and the Japanese presence was felt in cameras and sewing machines. Not infrequently the American manufacturer will find a domestic competitor among his leading rivals in the EEC. For example, General Motors and Ford are major protagonists in automobiles, and now Chrysler is on the scene as well. Pepsi-Cola and Coca-Cola are the chief competitors in cola drinks in Europe. Similar examples could be cited in chemicals, farm equipment, paper products, and other lines. In computers, International Business Machines Corporation leads the field, competing against almost the same American companies that it faces in the American market--plus European competition.

Frequently, American manufacturers beginning local production try to avoid locating in the country that is the "fief" of a major European producer--or where a competing American firm is strongly entrenched. Rather than tackle an established stronghold immediately, it is often desirable to build up a market in another country and later move from a position of strength. For example, two paper goods manufacturers are major competitors in the United States and both are now operating in the Common Market. The first one to produce in Europe located in France and Germany. The later arrival located in Belgium and Italy. They will probably be competing throughout the EEC in five or ten years, but each will probably have a particular strength in certain Member Countries. A more regional illustration is given by a manufacturer of durables, who is establishing production and marketing in Southern Italy. Only after a satisfactory market share is obtained there does the firm expect to invade Northern Italy, where the leading Italian producer dominates the market.

The effect of the Rome Treaty on competition was felt to be rather insignificant by most of the respondents. As to their own behavior, the American companies were acting in

accordance with American antitrust law and found this to be
a sufficient guarantee of proper conduct in the context of the
"Rules of Competition" in the treaty. There was rather general skepticism about the treaty's impact on European manufacturers. Many respondents said there had been little change
in the competitive philosophy or practices of their European
competitors or suppliers. The changes that had occurred
were attributed not to the treaty but to excess capacity and
the increase of international selling. Similar conclusions
were reached in a study by two British economists.[2] However, the American manufacturers agreed that the "Rule of
Competition" were an influence in the right direction; and some
were sanguine about their eventual positive impact.

Nature of the Increased Competition

As indicated in the chapter on pricing, there has been an
increase in price competition in the Common Market. The
American manufacturers usually contribute to this only as
a last resort because they would prefer to compete on other
grounds where they have greater advantages. The European
manufacturers are no more desirous of cutting prices than
the American, but the pressure of excess capacity and new
competition and the frequent absence of nonprice weapons
have often meant that they have been the leaders in increasing
price competition.

Nonprice competition has also increased in the Common
Market and is often the major change in the increasingly competitive environment. Occcasionally, cartel or collusive practices will hurt the American manufacturer; but the major competitive activities he has to adjust to in the EEC are the same
ones he faces in the American market. The European manufacturers now have greater financial resources and engage
in heavier promotion and more research and development leading to product innovation and differentiation. One U.S. consumer
goods marketer remarked that a new product used to give the
firm an edge for five years, but that this time was greatly reduced today in the EEC because of the aggressive product innovation of European competitors.

Many European manufacturers are now conducting marketing
research and have become more sophisticated, more aggressive marketers. They have not hesitated to copy successful

techniques of American companies, as was suggested by
Scitovsky: "The better industrial and commercial practices
are likely to displace the inferior ones; and the behavior and
habits of thought of the more ambitious, more pushing and
more ruthless are likely to prevail and be adopted by their
more easy-going competitors."[3] They have also used local
branches of American advertising agencies to benefit from
the latest American know-how in promotion and marketing
research. Today, of course, there are European agencies
which can offer services of a similar caliber.

Response of American Manufacturers

The pressure of sharper competition along with a greater
interest in Common Market business have led to many types
of adjustment by American manufacturers. The previous
chapters have discussed these in detail, as the purpose of the
study is to examine American manufacturers adaptation to
new conditions in the EEC. Organizational changes for European business were among the first adjustments. New top-
level personnel were assigned to the international division, and
there was decentralization of responsibility and functions to
Europe. Local manufacturing was begun or expanded. This
was accomplished primarily through wholly owned direct operations but partly through acquisitions, joint ventures, and
licensing. The last three types of operation were frequently
by firms newer in the European market.

Other types of adjustment included a "Europeanization"
of product planning, product line, promotion, pricing, and
other marketing functions. Marketing research activities
have been initiated or expanded, often after unhappy experiences in the market. Once American manufacturers decided that the European market was worth their best efforts,
they generally responded in a way sufficient to make themselves strong competitors. The Common Market and related
developments were strong inducements to put forth their best
efforts.

ADVANTAGES AND HANDICAPS OF
AMERICAN MANUFACTURERS

The American manufacturer in Europe has certain competitive handicaps in his operations. These arise primarily

from his foreignness and because he is less familiar with the
market than his European competitors. This lack of familiarity refers not only to customer wants and buying habits, but
also to the competitive environment and practice, government
regulations and attitudes, and other environmental factors
that affect a firm's approach to the market as well as its
ability to compete effectively. One aspect of the American's
foreignness is that national competitors have subtle and not-
so-subtle ways of getting their government on their side.

Offsetting these handicaps are other factors that can
make it possible for an American company to operate very
profitably in Europe. Even the foreign image may be an
asset if the firm's product is one that benefits from an American image. Such consumer products as cola drinks, chewing gum, and women's foundation garmets are in this category. Unfamiliarity with the market may also mean freedom
from traditional practices and viewpoints that are not suited
to a Europe of growing affluence and economic integration.
A new approach is often easier for a firm new to the market.

It should be noted, on the other hand, that a number of
American manufacturers are veteran operators in Europe and
have become as familiar with their market as the indigenous
firms. In fact, respondents of most such companies said that
one of their major competitive advantages was their long experience in Europe, leading to development of strong European
management, familiarity with the market, and well established
distribution systems. They felt that American firms coming
into the European market in very recent years had especially
great handicaps in acquiring local management, know-how,
and distribution.

American manufacturers establishing European operations in the late 1950's did indeed have great difficulty in
getting local know-how and distribution. This is one of the
chief reasons why most of the latecomers in the market entered into some kind of association with European firms,
usually by acquisition or joint venture. Without such a link-
age to European firms, many American newcomers would not
have been able to establish themselves merely on their particularly American strengths.

Once the American manufacturers have been able to overcome the lack of local knowledge and distribution, they are
likely to enjoy certain competitive advantages. Generally,
American firms have greater financial resources than their
European competitors. These resources enable American
companies to engage more heavily in promotion and other
forms of nonprice competition, to persevere in the market
in unprofitable periods, and to conduct more research, which
may lead to product innovation and technological superiority.
Much of the European fear of an American industrial "in-
vasion" was because of the great financial resources of American companies. This fear is something like that of the American independent grocers in the face of the growth of the giant
food chains in the 1930's.

An important advantage for many American firms in Europe derives from a special strength in some aspect of production.
Some find that their experience with mass production in America enables them to produce more efficiently than their European competitors who are less familiar with such techniques.
Indeed, the wise American manufacturer studies the competitive
cost situation before choosing his field of entry in the Common
Market so as to have such an advantage. [4]

Another production-related advantage claimed by many
American manufacturers in Europe is the superiority of their
quality-control programs. Producers of both consumer goods
and industrial goods said their products enjoyed the reputation of being purer, stronger, more exact, or more uniform
than similar European products because of strict quality-control programs.

A further product and production advantage of many American manufacturers is their long experience in a particular
line. While a patent position can be an important benefit, an
even greater edge is often given by proprietary knowledge acquired through extensive experience with certain products or
in working with particular industries. This special product
or application knowledge, if supported by continuing research,
can be the American company's major edge vis a vis European competitors. This resource of specialized knowledge is
apt to be more significant and lasting than possession of superior financial resources, though the latter may help to maintain the former.

A technological lead over European competitors was claimed by a number of American firms. This results both from specialized experience and continued heavy research and development activity. Of course, technological leadership is related to the other production advantages already mentioned: experience with mass production, quality control, patent position, and proprietary knowledge. These could be considered as aspects of technological leadership, although the term, as used here, refers more to the ability to bring out an advanced product. The Europeans have now become very concerned about this "technology gap."

Somewhat intangible and complex is the advantage given to the American firm in Europe because of its American and multinational operations. The American company operating in Europe gains from its experience in the large United States market, but frequently also benefits from its operations in other national markets. European competitors generally are national firms with national resources, whereas the American company can often call on global experience and resources. The trial of products and techniques in one country, successful or otherwise, adds to the firm's fund of knowledge and strengthens its competitive posture elsewhere. Furthermore, the operation of profit centers in many countries and environments should increase the amount of creative thinking done in the corporation.

Not least of the competitive advantages of American manufacturers is their generally greater customer orientation and consequent sophistication in marketing. Part of the reason for their advance here is the fact that a buyers' market existed in the United States before it came to Europe. Furthermore, their experience in marketing to the mass, affluent United States market trained them for an integrated, affluent Europe, where many consumption and marketing patterns are following earlier American experience. The extensive American use of marketing research means that investment, product, and marketing errors are minimized. Products are more likely to meet customer desires, and marketing activity is apt to be more effective than with most European competitors. The prudent American manufacturer moves from a position of strength in particular markets with particular products. By avoiding "me too" products, he reduces his vulnerability to European competition.

American manufacturers have generally been quicker to implement an EEC-wide approach in a more rational organization of both production and marketing. This places them in a stronger position as the Common Market becomes a practical reality. Their experience in the United States common market is an asset here.

The customer orientation already mentioned shows itself in many ways. It is evident in the products, promotion, and distribution of American manufacturers. It means greater missionary selling with intermediaries and in the industrial market extensive pre-sale and post-sale service. In fact, several manufacturers of industrial goods said their greatest advantage in the Common Market was their strong sales-service work and superior knowledge of product applications.

CONCLUSIONS

Competition has increased in the Common Market as expected, although European recovery was the major single cause and antedated the Rome Treaty. American manufacturers will frequently find American competitors among their chief rivals in Europe, but the major increase in competition is from the new strength and sophistication of European firms. The Rome Treaty has not yet been an important cause of the growth in competition except by introducing the customs union, which has led to a great rise in international selling. The "Rules of Competition" have had a rather small impact thus far.

American manufacturers face certain handicaps in the Common Market, arising primarily from foreignness. However, they may enjoy several competitive advantages making possible successful operations in the EEC. It should be noted that the several advantages indicated are a matter of degree and depend much on the particular situation facing the individual firm. While American firms can and do compete successfully in the EEC, they must first overcome their lack of familiarity with the market. Then, rather than assuming competitive superiority, they must choose their market niche after careful study and be ready to compete in the manner and degree required by the challenges and opportunities in the market.

European manufacturers generally are stronger than ever, and there are some who could give lessons to American manufacturers in international business. All this means that profit opportunities exist in Europe, but American firms can tap them only by dint of aggressive effort along with the help of their particular resources and advantages.

NOTES TO CHAPTER 8

1. Tibor Scitovsky, Economic Theory and Western European Integration (Stanford, Calif.: Stanford University Press, 1958), p. 20.

2. D. L. McLachlan and D. Swann, "Competition Policy in the Common Market," The Economic Journal, LXXIII, 289 (March, 1963), 54-79.

3. Scitovsky, op. cit., p. 23.

4. Raphael W. Hodgson and Hugo E. R. Uyterhoeven, "Analyzing Foreign Opportunities," Harvard Business Review, XL, 2 (March-April, 1962), 60-79.

CHAPTER **9** CONCLUSIONS

The primary goal of this study is to analyze and evaluate the impact of the Common Market on American manufacturers' marketing approach to the countries of the EEC. The adjustments made in particular marketing activities to achieve adaptation have been described. Since most of the chapters have their own concluding sections, the discussion here will be concerned with a broader consideration of the significance of American business adaptation to the Common Market since 1957.

There are several areas of interest that may be explored. One is the theory of economic integration in the light of these operations. Have such adaptations conformed to what would have been predicted? A second area of interest is the adaptability of American manufacturers to a changing international environment. Is American business able to survive and grow in dynamic international markets with anything like the success achieved domestically? A related question is the applicability of American marketing experience to the emerging situation in the Common Market.

A third area worthy of examination is the impact of American business on the Common Market and upon European manufacturers. While not the direct concern of the present study, it may be that this impact is the most important one. Although many incidents of European reaction to American operations are cited throughout the study, a more general evaluation will be given in this chapter.

THEORETICAL CONSIDERATIONS

In the theory of economic integration, there are three concepts directly related to the operations of American manufacturers in the EEC as discussed in this study. One is that there should be a reallocation and centralization of production in the Member Countries. A second related concept is that there should be a movement toward specialization of production, with an implied narrowing of the product line of the individual manufacturer. A third concept is the expectation of increased competition following economic integration.

Centralization of Production

This tendency was discussed at some length in Chapter 2. The theory must be judged as correct insofar as it points to the direction of change. There has been a reallocation and centralization of production by American manufacturers. Of those American companies who had more than one plant on the Continent at the time of the Rome Treaty, several have reallocated production with plants in particular countries specializing on a narrower product line. Some even operate in a product-by-plant basis. Other firms that have established new plants in the EEC produce a particular product for the whole Market rather than a complete line for a national market. These developments are strongest in industrial goods. This fact substantiates the expectation that the Common Market will become "common" first in this product area.

The theory, however, while showing the direction of change, does not explain the many instances where production has not been reallocated or rationalized. For many American firms, especially producers of consumer nondurable goods, production is still primarily for national markets. There are economic pressures for change in the way suggested by the theory, but there are also several noneconomic factors that continue to inhibit a more rational reallocation of production. Among these are diversity of national regulations, national purchasing preferences, different national tastes and habits, and, to some extent, management inertia. These counterpressures are so strong, in fact, that, even where production is centralized for the whole EEC, distribution channels and marketing organizations are invariably national.

While real-life frictions disturb the workings of the pure theoretical model (as is usually the case), the experience of American firms in the EEC cannot be said to contradict the theory, but only to show some roadblocks in the path it traces. Indeed, one would venture the guess that a similar study undertaken five years from the present writing (1966) would show much further progress along the road indicated on the theoretical "map," especially if there are improvements in transportation to parallel the dismantling of tariff barriers.

Specialization of Production

This topic is intimately related to the above discussion as one would expect the reallocation of production to lead to specialization, not only by plant but by producer. Competitive pressures would tend to force this change as well as the larger market--specialization being limited by the size of the market. The question is of interest to the present study because it implies a narrowing of the product line of American manufacturers and specialization according to comparative advantage.

The evidence found here is somewhat ambiguous but generally against the expectation of a narrower product line, as far as American firms are concerned. There are numerous examples of American firms dropping "me too" products to specailize on lines where they are strongest. On the whole, however, these companies have had expanding product lines in Europe. Almost all are selling more varieties of product than they did before the Rome Treaty.

When one analyzes the reasons, this fact is not too surprising. American manufacturers have increased both their desire and their ability to provide wider product lines in Europe. Their desire for greater European business arose from various causes, among them the "profit squeeze" in the United States in the late 1950's. Another was the realization that Western Europe was again becoming a major market--and more attractive because of economic integration. The "fashion" or "prestige" element in establishing or expanding European operations might also be mentioned.

The American firms' ability to sell wider product lines arises principally from their increased production facilities in Europe. This new capacity allows them to be competitive on more products than was the case with exports from America or their smaller previous plants. Where expansion comes through acquisition of a European manufacturer, his existing line is usually continued with new American products added. Further enabling the sale of a wider line are the greatly enlarged marketing staffs and promotional budgets of American companies.

Some additional pressures for expansion of the product line will be noted in passing: the typical desire to have the

same line in all countries, product development that adds
new items while existing ones do not "fade away" easily, and
the frequent possibility of getting more effective and efficient
distribution with a broader line.

Increased Competition

Economic integration should lead to increased competition
from two major sources: greater international sales by national producers and the entry of new firms attracted by the
opportunities in the enlarged market. The results in this instance are clear; there has been a notable rise in competition
in the EEC. Although the "Rules of Competition" in the Rome
Treaty have not yet had much impact, both European and
American manufacturers have had to become more aggressive
competitors. The entry of new "foreign" firms in each Member
Country has invigorated the competitive environment on a national as well as on an EEC level.

Since competition affects all the marketing activities of
the firm, this topic has been discussed in every chapter, with
particular consideration of competition itself in Chapter 8.
The major findings are that, while both American and European firms have contributed to sharpening the competitive
climate, the Americans emphasize nonprice competition while
the Europeans compete more on price. American companies
with their greater financial resources and marketing sophistication can rely relatively more on product development, promotion, and service. European companies often are unable
to do this and are forced to depend on price alone. The frequent presence of excess capacity increases the pressure for
price reduction.

In summary, it can be said that the theory of economic
integration is a useful guide to understanding business developments in the EEC. By itself, however, it can be quite misleading. What is necessary is a theoretical "road map" along
with some knowledge of the actual "terrain." With these two
elements, one can know the ultimate destination as well as
the obstacles in the way.

It must be emphasized that the conclusions here are limited
to American companies, which constitute a small part of total
manufacturing activity in the EEC. For a true test of the theory,

one would have to examine the operations of European manufacturers. That is beyond the scope of the present study.
The MSI study which touched briefly on this topic came to
rather ambiguous conclusions.[1]

AMERICAN MANUFACTURERS AS
INTERNATIONAL COMPETITORS

American industrial performance was the wonder of the
world during World War II. In the postwar period numerous
productivity teams came here to study American techniques,
and an American technical assistance program was started.
American manufacturers have performed well in the domestic
economy. How do they perform as international competitors?

Prior to World War II, American business involvement
abroad (apart from exports) was relatively limited, being
strongest in the extractive industries. Today, however,
American manufacturers are operating in all parts of the free
world, and especially in Western Europe. The present study
is revealing as to the international adaptability and strength
of these manufacturers.

Since one of the major purposes of the research is to
investigate this question, much about it has been included in
all previous chapters; and only a few general comments will
be made here. In response to new threats and opportunities
in world markets, major American manufacturers have responded in a variety of ways to assure themselves a strong
international position. One of the first and major steps was
organizational adjustment to cope with the new challenges.
Perhaps the most important aspect of this was the increase
in top-level attention to international business, because this led
in turn to its receiving more financial resources and high-
level personnel.

Another significant step was a change in location of supply for Western Europe. Once American companies became
really interested in Europe, they frequently established or
expanded European production sources to serve the market.
New production sources arose through licensing, joint ventures, or wholly owned operations, with the trend toward a
greater degree of ownership. With this larger participation

went increased attention to European business and consequent greater rewards.

All the marketing activities of American manufacturers in Europe have undergone varying degrees of adjustment. These changes were caused in part by changes in market conditions and in part by the new American interest in Western Europe. Product policy, promotion, and pricing were Europeanized. Distribution channels were studied for their suitability under the new conditions of supply. The use of marketing research was greatly expanded to find guidance in adjusting to dynamic markets. Collectively, these adjustments enabled the survival and growth of American companies in the EEC.

In their generally successful operations in the Common Market, American firms have several competitive advantages. Their technical and financial resources are usually mentioned first. Also important for most companies is their experience in marketing in America. In foreign operations, the question of conformity or innovation always arises. Rigid adoption of either extreme is usually wrong. American companies in Europe have made their share of costly mistakes, but they have learned from them. Their American experience helps to guide them in the right direction for today's-- and tomorrow's--European market. The United States is a common market, and experience here helps as a common market evolves in the EEC. Furthermore, the affluent buyers' market in America gives manufacturers a sophistication in marketing that   stands them in very good stead in the European buyers' market of rising affluence.

All in all, American manufacturers have shown themselves as worthy international competitors. They have entered unfamiliar markets against entrenched competition. In spite of difficulties and occasional reverses, they have generally established themselves as strong factors in the market, with a notable impact on both competitors and consumers. Their survival ability in international markets seems to be almost as good as in domestic markets, once they put their minds to it.

A NOTE ON THE ROLE OF AMERICAN
MANUFACTURERS IN THE COMMON MARKET

In the European Economic Community there has been a rising tide of criticism of United States investment in the Member Countries. Among American businessmen there has been increasing awareness of and sensitivity of this criticism. [2] To what extent is European hostility justified? What can American firms say in defense of their presence? It is the purpose of this section to evaluate the Common Market activities of American manufacturers in the light of over-all Community goals.

Within the EEC, there are often ambivalent feelings toward the presence of American manufacturers in the Member Countries. While the inflow of capital and technology usually associated with this investment is welcomed, the European business community frequently resents the increased competition--and even governments may fear the importance of the American role in particular industries. De Gaulle has been the most prominent critic though he speaks primarily just for France (or perhaps for de Gaulle). However, there are questioning voices in other Member Countries, and even among the EEC authorities. Robert Marjolin, vice-president of the EEC Commission, said:

> We think that slowing down American direct investment in the industrially developed countries would also contribute to the general health of our economies. It would be useful if the Community countries adopted a common attitude to these transactions. [3]

In evaluating the American presence in the Common Market, a variety of viewpoints could be taken. One could speak from the viewpoint of the American firms operating in Europe or from that of the host countries. One could discuss the benefits of free trade or the advantages of direct private investment. For example, the benefits of free, or freer, trade are acknowledged in the West; and expansion of trade is a goal of the Common Market, the European Free Trade Association, and the United States (as in the Trade Expansion Act of 1962). Economists have discussed the advantages of direct private investment, and the National Planning Association has a series of case studies showing the benefits of such investment to the host country.

Since the criticism has come from the EEC side and since the interests of the host countries should predominate, the viewpoint taken here is the interests of the Member Countries as affected by the operations of American manufacturers in the EEC. Specifically, what is intended here is to relate some of the concepts of free trade and private investment to the particular case of American manufacturers' activities in the EEC and the specific goals of the Common Market. If the EEC is to continue to progress and to be the key fact in tomorrow's Europe, it is reasonable to evaluate the activities of American firms in the light of over-all Community goals, rather than in the light of more parochial national goals or criticisms.

While American operations will be judged in the light of the interests of the Community, it is not implied that American firms pay particular attention to Community welfare in making decisions. Indeed, there is little to suggest that they are motivated by other than profit (or other corporate goals) when operating in Europe. Along with Adam Smith, most American executives reject altruism or the public good as a major influence upon operations. Nevertheless, it is interesting to examine whether the profit-seeking activities of American manufacturers do, in fact, contribute to the attainment of Common Market goals. If this is true, the EEC should have a more favorable attitude toward these activities than in the opposite case. Furthermore, criticisms of particular countries or industry groups should be considered in the light of over-all Community benefits.

Common Market Goals

The goals of the EEC are indicated in the Rome Treaty, which established the Common Market. The major objectives of the Community founders are stated in Article 2 of the treaty. The English translation of this says:

It shall be the aim of the Community, by establishing a Common Market and progressively approximating the economic policies of the Member States, to promote throughout the Community a harmonious development of economic activities, a continuous and balanced expansion, an increased stability, an accelerated raising of the standard of living and closer relations between Member States.[4]

A further objective is the creation and maintenance of a competitive environment as indicated in the well-known Articles
85 and 86. These then are the goals which provide the frame-
work for evaluating American manufacturers in the Common
Market.

"Throughout the Community"

One of the objectives of the EEC is to equalize standards
of living and working throughout the Community. This means,
of course, working towards the highest rather than the lowest
common denominators. It is desired that progress achieved
be generalized among all Member Countries. The operations
of American manufacturers appear to contribute to the attainment of this goal. Along with such internationalists as Unilever and Nestle, American manufacturers tend both to produce
and to market in several Member Countries.

Multinational Production. In this study, over a third of the
firms were producing in five Member Countries and the median
firm was producing in three. While this was a rather small
sample of large firms, another recent study of 2,042 United
States companies reiterates this spread of American manufacturing activity among Member Countries.[5] This geographical distribution of American manufacturing is certainly in
line with the Community goal of equalizing working conditions,
for American companies tend to follow the same personnel
practices and methods of operations from country to country.
Furthermore, since they tend to pay somewhat higher wages
and try to provide better conditions and benefits than their
European competitors, their presence results in pressure
for improving working conditions throughout the Community.

Employee-training programs perhaps deserve special
mention as an equalizing and upgrading force in the Community. Whether these take the form of technical schooling
in a computer firm or even the special training of driver-
salesmen in a soft drink company or missionary sales training by a chewing gum manufacturer, they usually represent
an improvement over current practices in the Member
Countries. When these American programs and practices
are successful, they tend to be further generalized through
imitation by competitors throughout the Common Market.
Andre Siegfried, writing in the early 1950's, suggested that

Europe could not use American methods to achieve prosperity. [6]
To some extent, at least, American manufacturers in Europe
have proved him wrong.

A special aspect of the generalization of progress is the
Community concern for depressed areas. Both the EEC and
individual Member Countries have incentive programs to encourage establishment of business in these regions. Whether
it be in the Italian Mezzogiorno or a depressed area of Belgium,
American manufacturers have responded relatively more than
European firms in establishing plants. While the particular
tax and other inducements have been the self-interested motivation of the American response, the result is nonetheless
to further this part of the EEC program.

Multinational Marketing. In their marketing activities, American manufacturers are even more thorough in covering the
Common Market; they're selling in more countries than they're
producing in. Though their product line occasionally differs
from country to country, American firms generally offer advanced and American-type products (in which they have a competitive edge). They have little chance of success unless they
can offer something different, or better, or cheaper than is
already there. Therefore, the products they market usually
represent an increase in the variety and quality available to
consumers in the EEC.

Because of experience in the great U. S. common market and their desire to enjoy the benefits of standardization in
Europe, American companies offer the same products in all
Member Countries insofar as possible. This offering of
similar products in different countries tends to equalize standards of living. Thus, production or consumption advances
realized through the activities of American manufacturers are
indeed generalized "throughout the Community" because of
the multicountry operations of American firms.

"A Harmonious Development of Economic Activities,
a Continuous and Balanced Expansion" and "An
Accelerated Raising of the Standard of Living."

The contribution of American manufacturers to these goals
of development, growth, and prosperity can be considered under
four headings: capital, technology, marketing skills, and
management skills.

Capital. The obtaining of capital resources is crucial to any program of growth and development. This is true both for countries (whether underdeveloped or advanced) and for firms. Even after more than a decade of European recovery and expansion, capital is not in abundant supply in Europe. Many European firms have complained about the competitive advantage given to American manufacturers by their great capital resources. However, this very capital has been a valuable contribution to the growth of the over-all European economy. As Michael Blumenthal noted in a recent speech, the book value of United States direct investment in the EEC rose from $1.9 billion in 1958 to $5.4 billion in 1964.[7]

The Common Market countries have thus been major beneficiaries of this investment for the past several years. This capital flow has had sound economic justification. The slow-down in the American economy in the late 1950's and political instability in Latin America combined with rapid growth and economic integration in Europe made the Continent the most attractive investment outlet in almost any analysis. It should be noted, however, that the EEC, as well as individual Member Countries, had a very good propaganda program, which further encouraged American investment there. Second thoughts about the American presence came only after its impact became significantly apparent. The productive role played by this capital is usually well recognized by the host governments. However, particular national manufacturers do not welcome the extra competition it brings, even though it does foster the growth and development of the over-all Community.

Technology. Directly related to the supply to capital in direct private investment is the inflow of technology. This technology may be "frozen" in the form of machinery and equipment or "loose" in the form of special techniques and proprietary knowledge. Whichever form it takes, this inflow of technology into Europe is likely to be new to Europe or an improvement over what is already available. This is true not because all American technology or equipment is better than the European, but because the prudent American manufacturer will tend to choose a market niche where he has a technological edge.

On "me too" products where European technology is as good as the American, the American manufacturers generally leave production to Europeans. As one executive noted: "We do not enter a product in a market unless it has at least one point of demonstrable superiority over competing products." This philosophy is held by many American manufacturers.

American technology enters Europe primarily through direct investment, though licensing is not unimportant. A related benefit in direct investment is the American practice of subcontracting. European manufacturers generally keep as much work in-house as possible, whereas American firms do a lot of subcontracting.[8] This practice serves to upgrade European technical skills and to disseminate further American technology in Europe. While difficult to measure, this influx of new American technology probably has contributed importantly to the "development of economic activities" as well as to the desired economic expansion and rising standards of living.

Marketing Skills. Before World War II, the cartel philosophy was strong in Europe, and most countries were suffering from the great economic depression. In the first postwar decade, the emphasis was on reconstruction and a sellers' market prevailed. These are some of the historical reasons why a consumer or market orientation is not well developed among European manufacturers generally. This was noted by Scitovsky[9] in the mid-1950's and reaffirmed in a 1963 study of European manufacturers.[10] The prevailing orientation of the average European firm was toward the physical product and production processes rather than toward determining market desires and how to satisfy them.

In the more competitive American economy, where a buyers' market existed earlier, American manufacturers had become rather strongly market-oriented, engaging much more in such marketing activities as promotion, marketing research, and continuous product development. A high degree of affluence with rising discretionary income reinforced the need for such activities. American firms operating in Europe in the late 1950's found conditions becoming more like those in the American market. They found themselves in the "right place" at the "right time." Their marketing sophistication usually proves to be one of their important competitive advantages in the Common Market. This was reiterated time and again by American executives in this study.

Today, European business has become quite marketing-minded; and American firms have played an important role in this. First, American manufacturers in their not insignificant operations in the EEC have tended to apply the same marketing philosophy and activities as in America, insofar as conditions permit. This is done through the American executives and staff working in Europe as well as through extensive training of European personnel, both in Europe and in America. Second, competition has forced many European firms to adopt successful marketing practices employed by American companies. In a very real sense, American manufacturers constitute an important group of marketing educators in Europe. It can be said that in Europe, marketing is being learned much less in schools of business administration than "on the job" and in the competitive market. American advertising agencies also have been influential in teaching marketing techniques.

This increase in marketing orientation and sophistication contributes to the Common Market goals of development and raising standards of living. It can reveal new avenues of market opportunity and help assure that the production and marketing processes yield greater utility to consumers. New products on the market will more accurately reflect just what consumers want, both as to the product and its marketing. This increased utility obtained in the market is equivalent to a rise in living standards, even though it isn't necessarily reflected in GNP.

Management Skills. There are varying degrees of competence among European managers, just as there are among American managers. In Europe, however, family management is found to a greater extent than in America, where professional management of industry is predominant. In Germany, for example, entrepreneurship is generally considered as a calling that can't really be taught. The many changes occurring in Europe-- economic growth and integration, rapid technological change-- have almost overwhelmed many European managers, who are unable to cope with the new environment. What is often needed in the "new" Europe is a new type of manager, or an upgrading of the skills of the old manager.

American manufacturers have made contributions to raising the level of management skill in the EEC and thus further aided the "development of economic activities." This contribution to European management has come in several ways. One is through their direct operations in Europe. Of course, not all American management is better than European management; but it is generally the best, most professionally managed American companies that are operating in Europe--those that can compete best and contribute most. What is referred to here is not the individual American manager abroad, but the over-all practices of American companies. Individual managers obviously vary in competence. [11] Their example and innovations are frequently imitated by European firms. Many respondents noted that product or marketing innovations made by their firms were quickly copied by alert European competitors as soon as they proved successful.

Managerial education is provided in more direct ways also. American companies train their European managers much as they do their American managers. There is on-the-job training in Europe and frequently special experience or training in America. One equipment manufacturer has a management school for all of Europe located in the Netherlands. Managers come and spend a whole month together. Another equipment firm has a similar operation in England that is open to its European dealers as well as company personnel. A major licensor trains its licensees and their personnel, and an automotive firm has an expert management-training team traveling around to help all of its franchised dealers. Thus, the management-training activities aren't limited to the American manufacturers' own personnel.

A more subtle way in which management upgrading is done is through the activities of equipment and computer firms. When they sell equipment or "systems," they are teaching new problem-solving approaches to management--and usually training special personnel also. Because of the global experience of these American firms, they are able to give the most advanced techniques to their European customers.

In the immediate postwar period, European productivity teams visited America to study techniques and methods. Today, American manufacturers are giving the benefit of their example and training on the spot in Europe. This on-the-spot experience combined with competitive pressures is probably much more effective than the visits of the earlier period.

It seems evident that the Common Market goals of development, growth, and prosperity are benefiting considerably from American manufacturers' important contributions of capital, technology, and marketing and management skills.

"Closer Relations Between Member States."

Greater political, economic, and social unity is certainly not least among EEC goals, though it is last named in Article 2. This unity is not formed by fiat or treaties but must be woven from many threads of common progress and joint endeavor. The multicountry EEC operations of American manufacturers make a useful contribution to "closer relations between Member States."

For one thing, American manufacturers are much more likely to consider the whole EEC as a market unit than is the average European firm, which tends to wear nationalist glasses. While many American companies also still have national operations, there is an important difference in emphasis and approach. National operations may continue to be necessary for some, but the desire and planning of American firms is for a single market operation as soon as feasible. This integrated Common Market-wide approach helps to unify the economies of the Member Countries and brings closer personal relations as well.

There is another way in which American manufacturers contribute to closer relations on a personal basis. Many have regular meetings of managerial or other personnel from different national subsidiaries. In some cases, there are even meetings for distributors from different countries. (The Europe-wide training programs of some American firms have been cited above.) Two examples can be cited here. A food company has subsidiaries in all EEC countries. Just ten years ago, the various managers "never saw each other and each went his own way." Now they meet together four times a year to discuss common problems and make some decisions as a body. Furthermore, in this same company, the top marketing people from these subsidiaries hold their own quarterly joint meetings. At an informal level, a soft drink manufacturer noted that its bottlers from one country make a point of visiting its bottlers in other countries when traveling abroad. Europe-wide or international house organs also help to stimulate interest in activities in other Member Countries.

It may be noted that the Rome Treaty talks of "closer relations between Member States" whereas I have considered primarily economic relations between firms and personal relations
between citizens of different countries. However, these different aspects are intimately and necessarily related. Closer
relations will not be achieved by intergovernmental agreements
or laws. Such agreements can be effective only if a majority
of the citizens support them, i.e., only if the political and
economic situation is favorable. When this happens, European
integration will be a fait accompli practically as well as legally.

An example may clarify this point. American experience
with Prohibition is a relevant illustration, but there is a better
one in recent European history. The European Defense Community was a rather straightforward political attempt to unify
Europe. The plan failed because of a lack of popular support,
especially in France. It was this failure that led the pro-
ponents of a united Europe to try for unity through a grass-
roots economic approach such as has been mentioned here.
From these efforts was born the European Economic Community with the same political goal of "closer relations between Member States." [12]

As this discussion has suggested, the Rome Treaty's goal
of greater unity and harmony among Member States is very
much in agreement with the desires of American manufacturers
operating in Europe. The American firms in their day-to-
day management as well as in their long-range planning are a
positive force for the realization of this goal. Their increasingly integrated and unified European operations and their part
in bringing closer personal relations should be counted in
their favor when evaluating their desirability as citizens of
the Common Market.

Competition

Whereas maintenance of competition has long been official American policy, that has not been true in Europe. Today, however, this is formally the case for the EEC as a whole.
Indeed, the "Rules of Competition" in Articles 85 and 86 are
strongly reminiscent of our own antitrust laws. Nevertheless,
this is another instance of where the mere insertion of articles
into the treaty does not ensure realization of the benefits desired. In fact, most observers feel that Articles 85 and 86 have

had rather small impact. In spite of this, competition has increased notably in the Common Market; and the American presence has been an important cause.

The arrival of new American firms in Europe means an increase in the number of competitors. More important than mere numbers, however, is the quality of American competition. The American manufacturers in Europe are usually large, efficient producers and can exert competitive pressure out of proportion to their numbers. Because of their fear of, and conformance with United States antitrust laws, they are less likely to be members of cartels or other restrictive agreements. In other words, they are more competitive than the average European firms and more likely to disturb a quiescent competitive situation. The fact that they are newcomers in the market also makes this more probable.

While American firms are not especially leaders in price competition in Europe, they add a new strength and dimension to nonprice competition. Greater promotional activity, innovations in distribution and service, and consumer-oriented product development characterize American manufacturers' operations in the EEC. Several observers have noted the apparent reluctance of European manufacturers to use all these methods of nonprice competition.[13] However, as American companies have succeeded through the use of these methods, European firms have had to become more agressive in spite of themselves.

American investment in the Common Market has been estimated at about 2 per cent of the total. This is rather small amount, but the figure is very misleading as to the significance of the investment. Some European competitors may consider it as the "one bad apple which spoils the whole barrel." In any case, it is a crucial and catalytic 2 per cent having an influence on the competitiveness of the environment far greater than the figure suggests. (Of course, the 2 per cent is an average; and the American role in particular industries may be many times greater.) It is fair to say that the American companies constitute one of the major competitive forces in the Common Market. While this is disquieting to many European firms, it is nevertheless in accordance with the desires of the founders of the EEC, who specifically sought the benefits of competition for the whole Community.

A <u>caveat</u> should be sounded in closing. This analysis is not meant to suggest that American firms are the sole salvation of the Common Market. There are many political, economic, and social factors contributing to the progress of the EEC, including the activities of large European manufacturers operating internationally. What has been suggested, however, is that the American manufacturers in Europe, while pursuing selfish corporate goals are at the same time an important force helping to create the Common Market along the lines envisioned by the framers of the Rome Treaty. Because of their unique strengths and advantages and their EEC-wide approach, American manufacturers are probably contributing more to the realization of the Common Market than are most European firms.

A second <u>caveat</u> relates to the individual American manufacturer in the EEC. I don't want to imply that all are paragons of business virtue. Some have occasionally acted in ways that offended not only the sensitivities, but also the legitimate interests of the host countries. Such actions bring justified criticism.

It is incumbent on American companies to be very circumspect in their behavior. This may require even going the "second mile" in today's critical environment. Guest companies will not always be allowed that which is permitted to national firms. A reputation for good citizenship is something that is earned slowly--and continuously. Such a reputation may be the vital factor in the continuation of American operations in the Common Market.

NOTES TO CHAPTER 9

1. Marketing Science Institute, <u>Marketing Development in the European Economic Community</u> (New York: McGraw-Hill Book Co., Inc., 1964), pp. 91-96, 98-100, 116-22.

2. Richard Austin Smith, "European Nationalism Threatens U. S. Investment," <u>Fortune</u>, August, 1965, pp. 126 ff.

3. European Community, April, 1965, p. 5.

4. Treaty Establishing the European Economic Community (London: Her Majesty's Stationery Office, 1962), p. 3.

5. New Foreign Business Activity of U.S. Firms--54 Months--1960-64 (New York: Booz, Allen & Hamilton, Inc., 1965), pp. 20, 21.

6. Andre Siegfried, "Can Europe Use American Methods?" Foreign Affairs, July, 1962, pp. 660-68.

7. Cited in EFTA Reporter, May 9, 1966, p. 7.

8. See Edward A. McCreary, The Americanization of Europe (Garden City, N.Y.: Doubleday & Co., Inc., 1964), pp. 77-79.

9. Tibor Scitovsky, Economic Theory and Western European Integration (Stanford, Calif.: Stanford University Press, 1958), pp. 22-32.

10. MSI, op. cit., p. 29.

11. McCreary, op. cit., pp. 183-96.

12. Stuart de la Mahotiere, The Common Market (London: Hodder & Staughton, Ltd., 1961), pp. 11-15.

13. Scitovsky, op. cit., p. 122.

I

Anonymity was promised the respondents, so no identification will be made. Except for names, however, a rather full description is given below. There were ten respondents from the industrial goods field, eleven consumer nondurable firms, and four in consumer durables. However, one consumer nondurables firm and one industrial goods firm were also active in consumer durables, making six firms selling in that category. Most of the consumer durables firms also had important industrial markets. The diversification of the large firms prevents mutually exclusive categories.

Products Marketed in Europe by Respondent Firms

Consumer Nondurables

1. Cosmetics and toiletries for men and women.

2. Food and beverage products: canned fruits and vegetables, cookies, crackers and snack items, cake mixes, puddings, chewing gum, soft drinks, and soups.

3. Foundation garments: bras and girdles.

4. Photographic film and supplies.

5. Proprietary medicines.

6. Tissues, napkins, and other household and personal paper products.

7. Waxes and polishes for home and car.

Consumer Durables

1. Automobiles.

2. Cameras and projectors.

3. Floor polishers and other miscellaneous personal and home appliances.

4. Flooring and ceiling material.

5. Refrigerators and washing machines.

6. Sewing machines.

7. Televisions, phonographs.

8. Tires.

Industrial Goods

1. Business machines, including computers.

2. Chemicals--a wide range.

3. Diesel engines.

4. Drugs (pharmaceuticals).

5. Electrical equipment up to heavy installations.

6. Electronic equipment and components.

7. Elevators.

8. Locks and hardware.

9. Materials-handling equipment.

10. Packaging and cartons.

11. Plastics.

12. Synthetic fibers.

13. Tractors and full line of farm equipment.

14. Trucks.

Further Information on Firms in Sample

Length of Time Selling in the Common Market Countries

Nineteen of the respondent firms were selling in Western Europe before World War II, and seven of these were there already before World War I. The respondent firms thus reflect the historically predominant role of the large corporation in international business.

The six remaining firms began selling in Western Europe after World War II, and two of these began after 1950. Of those going in more recently, three were in the consumer goods field and three produced industrial goods.

Size of Firms by Total Sales and Common Market Sales

Except for one firm, total sales were obtained from annual reports. Common Market sales were given by about half of the respondents; and the other figures were estimated by the writer from figures on physical volume, percentages given by the respondents, and other indications. (Figures for 1963)

Total Sales	Companies
Over $1 billion	7
$500 million - $1 billion	6
$100 million - $499 million	11
Under $100 million	1
	25

EEC Sales	Companies
$150 - over $500 million	4
$50 - $149 million	4
$10 - $49 million	12
$2 - $9 million	5
	25

Common Market Sales as Per Cent Total Sales

Per Cent	Companies
11 - 20	5
6 - 10	9
1 - 5	11
	25

Manufacturing Facilities in the Common Market

At the time of the survey, all the respondent firms were manufacturing within the EEC, either by licensing or directly. Given here is the time of establishment of manufacturing in the Common Market (as opposed to plants in England).

Manufacturing Started in the EEC	Companies
Pre-World War I	5
1920 to 1940	3
1946 to 1956	9
1957 to 1962	8
	25

Almost one third of the respondents began manufacturing in the Common Market in 1957 or after. This, plus the fact that all the others have expanded their operations since 1957, suggests that integration has been an encouraging factor.

Investment in the Common Market

Very little factual data could be obtained as to the increase in these firms' investment in the EEC since 1957 or their EEC investment compared to total investment. However, over one third of the respondents did report EEC investment as ten per cent or more of total corporate investment.

For firms with licensing and joint-venture arrangements, relative investment figures would be misleading as to extent of EEC involvement. In such arrangements (and with exports), a sizable business can be carried on with relatively small capital investment in the EEC.

Profitability of Common Market Operations

Very little factual data was obtainable here either. This
was expected, but the question is of interest because one reason for undertaking operations in the EEC is presumably the
profit motive. Therefore, the evaluations of the respondents
will be noted.

Two of the respondents would not comment on this in any
way. Of the twenty-three who did, nine said Common Market
operations were still less profitable than North American
operations, seven found them more profitable, and seven found
profitability about the same in both places.

For the nine firms (four industrial goods, five consumer
goods) with relatively less profitable EEC activities, the ex
post profit figures must have been lower than the ex ante calculations. Three firms expected profits to improve as soon
as their operations were well-established. They felt that they
hadn't reached the takeoff stage there since they were quite
new in the market. Three of the largest respondent firms
found that greater competition (with a higher number of competitors and excess capacity) was hurting their profits. This was
combined in two cases with a lower degree of profit orientation among national competitors, especially where governments
owned or subsidized an industry. It was felt that in the long
run a rationalization of the industry would improve the situation.

For many firms the profitability story varied both by
product and by country. Generally, where operations were
new and/or national competition strong, profits were lower.
Where the firm was well-established and/or local competition
was weak, profits were good. One respondent admitted that
his company had built a large plant in one country without
adequate research and this was still hurting them. A few
others hinted at a similar problem. One firm wrote off several million dollars in losses in 1963 as a continuing cost of
late entry into the EEC. This was said to be part of the investment required to put the business on a sound footing for
the future.

Many other factors affect the profit picture also. On licensing operations, returns are not comparable with domestic

sales. One firm operating primarily through exports sold at the same f.o.b. plant price for both United States and foreign sales. It figured, however, that the extra foreign sales incurred lower marginal costs in production. Another firm selling industrial goods found its EEC operations more profitable from 1957-61, but the American side more profitable in 1962-63 when the United States economy was picking up again. A pharmaceutical firm said the EEC business was more profitable, but this was partly because all the basic research and development was done in the United States and not charged against EEC sales.

The Common Market was pictured as a great new market in the publicity and articles in the business press. While the EEC is a market that most large American firms cannot ignore, it is not a guaranteed profit opportunity as these findings show. One third of respondent firms were (1964) experiencing relatively unfavorable profit results. A few were still writing off losses after several years in the Market. While most intended to persist, one noted that "profits will have to rise if we're to stay in the Market." The day of "cream skimming" seems to be past in Europe, and successful entry and perseverance more than ever depend on careful analysis of the particular situation facing the firm. These remarks shouldn't be interpreted as a warning to stay away from the Common Market. They emphasize rather the need for care and diligence in entering it.

BIBLIOGRAPHY

Books

Allen, Frederick Lewis. The Big Change: America Transforms Itself. New York: Harper and Brothers, 1952.

Balassa, Bela. The Theory of Economic Integration. Homewood, Ill.: Richard D. Irwin, Inc., 1961.

Benoit, Emile. Europe at Sixes and Sevens: The Common Market, the Free Trade Association, and the United States. New York: Columbia University Press, 1961.

Commer, Heinz. Business Practice in the Common Market. New York: Frederick A. Praeger, 1963.

Dewhurst, J. Frederick, Coppock, John O., Yates, P. Lamartine, and Associates. Europe's Needs and Resources. New York: The Twentieth Century Fund, 1961.

Dunn, S. Watson (ed.). International Handbook of Advertising. New York: McGraw-Hill Book Co., Inc., 1964.

Fayerweather, John. Management of International Operations. New York: McGraw-Hill Book Co., Inc., 1960.

Granick, David. The European Executive. Garden City, N.Y.: Doubleday & Co., Inc., 1962.

Howard, John A. Marketing: Executive and Buyer Behavior. New York: Columbia University Press, 1963.

Humphrey, Don D. The United States and the Common Market --A Background Study. New York: Frederick A. Praeger, 1962.

Jeffreys, James B., and Knee, Derek. Retailing in Europe: Present Structure and Future Trends. London: Macmillan & Co., Ltd.

Kramer, Roland L. International Marketing. 2d ed. Cincinnati: Southwestern Publishing Company, 1964.

Mahotiere, Stuart de la. The Common Market. London: Hodder & Stoughton, Ltd., 1961.

Marketing Science Institute. Marketing Development in the European Economic Community. New York: McGraw-Hill Book Co., 1964.

McCreary, Edward A. The Americanization of Europe. Garden City, N.Y.: Doubleday & Co. Inc., 1964.

Nicholas, A.H. and Wilson, Aubrey. The Changing Pattern Of Distribution. London: Business Publications Limited, 1958.

Phelps, D. Maynard and Westing, J. Howard. Marketing Management, Rev. ed. Homewood, Ill.: Richard D. Irwin, Inc., 1960.

Robbins, W. David (ed.). Successful Marketing at Home and Abroad. Chicago: American Marketing Association, 1958.

Robinson, Richard D. International Business Policy. New York: Holt, Rinehart and Winston, 1963.

Scitovsky, Tibor. Economic Theory and Western Europe Integration. Stanford, Calif.: Stanford University Press, 1958.

Articles, Reports, and Monographs

American Management Association, Inc. Marketing Research in International Operations. AMA Management Report No. 53. New York: American Management Association, Inc., 1960.

Booz, Allen & Hamilton Inc. The Emerging World Enterprise. New York: Booz, Allen & Hamilton Inc., 1962.

_____. New Foreign Business Activity of U.S. Firms--54 Months--1960-64. New York: Booz, Allen & Hamilton Inc., 1965.

Economic Unity in Europe: Programs and Problems. New York: National Industrial Conference Board, 1960.

Lipsey, R. G. "The Theory of Customs Union: A General Survey," The Economic Journal, LXX, 279 (September, 1960), 496-513.

Marting, Elizabeth (ed.). The European Common Market: New Frontier for American Business. New York: American Management Association, Inc., 1958.

McGraw-Hill. Survey of Overseas Operations of U.S. Companies. New York: McGraw-Hill Book Co. Inc., 1960, 1963, 1966.

McLachlan, D. L. and Swann, D. "Competition Policy in the Common Market," The Economic Journal, LXXIII, 289 (March, 1963), 54-79.

Producing for European Markets. London: British Productivity Council, 1961.

Solving International Pricing Problems. New York: Business International, 1965.

Treaty Establishing the European Economic Community. London: Her Majesty's Stationery Office, 1962.

Periodicals

The following periodicals were reviewed for the period 1957-1966 and provided both general background and specific data for the study.

Advertising Age.

Business Abroad.

Business Europe.

Business International.

Business Week.

The Economist (London).

Entreprise (Paris).

European Community.

Export Trade.

Fortune.

German International.

Harvard Business Review.

The International Advertiser.

International Commerce.

The Journal of Marketing.

Monthly Economic Letter   (First National City Bank of New York).

Nation's Business.

Report on Western Europe   (Chase Manhattan Bank).

Retail News Letter (Paris).

Sales Management.

The Wall Street Journal.

ABOUT THE AUTHOR

Vern Terpstra is Associate Professor of International Business at the Graduate School of Business Administration, The University of Michigan. He previously taught marketing and international business at the Wharton School of the University of Pennsylvania. He has been a consultant on international studies at the Marketing Science Institute in Philadelphia.

Professor Terpstra lived and traveled in Europe in 1951-53 and was in Congo (Kinshasa) as Director of a Normal School from 1953-61. He is co-author of Marketing Development in the European Economic Community and has published several articles in the field of international business.

Professor Terpstra received his Ph.D. from The University of Michigan and has also studied at the University of Brussels.